Your Word:
Our Songs

Devotions for a Musician's Heart

By: **Shonnon Klassen**

Dedication

This devotional is dedicated to all who have encouraged my love of music, entrusted me with opportunities to lead in worship, and directed my heart to Jesus and His Word, and cherish the hope of His appearing.

Preface

Wondering what this devotional is about?

Here you go: A friend once called me a "worshipper," and she was right. Worshiping in a corporate setting is my joy. I try to be aware of God's presence in my everyday life and live in a way that brings glory to Him.

I am also a musician. I make no claims to brilliance, but I have several years of vocal training, play a couple of instruments, and majored in vocal music in college. So music, for me, is an important part of how I express my worship.

However, though I love to listen to teaching, I struggle with sitting down with God's Word and learning for myself. It's important, I know, but how do I stay motivated to stick with it for more than a couple of weeks at a time?

One day, while cleaning machines at my ice cream shop (yes, I have one of those), I was thinking, "I wonder if there is a devotional that is for people like me? From one musician's heart to another, that is true to scripture but draws in great worship music that points the heart to God?" I couldn't find one that was more than 10 days long.

So here we are... This series of devotionals is not about the music; it is about God and His Word to us.

I wrote these devotionals as I was studying God's Word. You are coming along with me as I learn and grow, and dig into the passages. Sometimes, I used a concordance to find a verse or phrase I was looking for. Sometimes, when a particularly difficult idea was in front of me, I went to trusted sources to help me understand it better. Anytime I did, you would find a note that says "Other Resources." You should do the same!

God may bring another verse or passage, or a question to mind as you are learning with me. Find it! Study it! My thoughts are definitely not God's thoughts, and He may have something to teach you that is just for you that day.

At the end of many of these devotions, you may find several questions. Some are rhetorical; we've already answered them, and you need to think about them more. Some are for us to answer within ourselves. What is God wanting me to learn, personally, today? A few may be questions that I don't have answers for yet. Maybe they will be answered as we continue to study, or maybe we will have to wait until we can ask Jesus face to face!

Sometimes, scripture reminds me of a song. Sometimes the song reminds me of a passage in the Bible. Some of the songs are familiar, some are new to me and probably to you. There might even be a couple that seem kind of silly. But the purpose of each combination of God's Word and our songs is to draw you closer to God, lift your heart in worship, or help you remember something from His Word.

The title of this book, "Your Word; Our Songs," comes from Psalm 119:54:

"Your statutes have been my songs in the house of my sojourning."

My prayer for each person who has this in their hand is that as you travel your road in this life, you will always have God's Word and a song in your heart.

- *Shonnon.*

How to Use This Book

I have used the English Standard Version for all of my Bible references.

You will need access to YouTube or Spotify.

I would recommend that you read the passage of the Bible first, then read the written devotional. Think about how it relates to the scripture.

Then listen to the song. If you search for what is notated, it should take you right to the correct song. Praise Him. Let His Word sink into your heart.

Take some time to pray. Perhaps the Spirit brought something to mind that you need to obey, or confess, or do. Lay your burdens on the table and give them to Jesus.

Matthew 7:21-23

One of my pastors often reminded his congregation that the scariest passage in the Bible is these three short verses.

There are two different groups of people here: Those who do the will of God the Father and those who think they are doing the will of the Father. Those who think they are doing the right things are upset because when it's time to enter the kingdom, they are rejected.

But why? "I did this and that in your name." And Jesus says, "I never knew you."

When talking about evangelism, the question that is often asked is, "Do you know Jesus?"

But in the church, perhaps we should be asking each other, "Does Jesus know you?"

How do we figure out if Jesus knows us?

"God knows those who love Him." (1 Corinthians 8:3)

"Do you seek Him?" (1 Chronicles 28:9)

"Are you aware of God's presence and that He knows your thoughts?" (Psalm 139:1-2)

"Do you have a sense of His calling and adoption over you?" (Galatians 1:15)

"Do you know that you are Jesus' friend and understand what he is doing? Or do you only see yourself as his servant?" (John 15:14-16)

A relationship with Christ isn't just about doing things, even in His name. It's about knowing and being known by Him.

Song: Nothing Else + The Heart of Worship

Kari Jobe, Lydia S. Marrow, Kristene DiMarco

Matthew 7:24-27

In March of 2023, we were in Florida, and we decided to spend a day at Daytona Beach. Our hotel wasn't fancy, but it was on the beach! I woke up early and went for a walk on the shore during the sunrise. The view was spectacular. Once the sun was up, I turned around and started back to the hotel, and I began to look more closely at the hotels and businesses looking out over the ocean.

It was 5 months after Hurricane Nicole had devastated Florida. The hurricane had taken enormous amounts of sand off the beach and swept it out to sea. The seaward sides of buildings had windows and doors boarded up, and I could see that the corners of some buildings had dropped a couple of feet as the foundations had been destroyed. Several of the hotel swimming pools had their entire foundation swept out from underneath and were broken in half. Retaining walls were rubble.

At the very end of the Sermon on the Mount, Jesus tells a short parable about wise people who build houses on rocks and foolish people who build on sand. When a hurricane hits, it becomes very easy to tell who is wise and who is foolish. The difference between the two groups? Those who obey Jesus and those who don't.

Psalm 19:14 calls God our Rock.

Psalm 95:1 He is the Rock of our salvation.

Eph 2:20-21 Jesus is the Cornerstone of the church and our lives.

Building our lives on the Rock of Jesus and obeying him is the only way to have stability and security. Building on sand might give great views and easy access to an ocean of things that look fun, but when the storms come, and they will come, I would rather be secured to the Rock.

The Rock Won't Move - Vertical Worship

Philippians 1:18-26

My Great Auntie Alice believed firmly that funerals for believers in Jesus were to be home-going celebrations. You don't wear black to a party. She consistently chose the brightest, prettiest thing in her closet. At one brother's funeral, she wore a chiffon dress with yellow, orange, and red flowers. At my great-grandmother's funeral, she wore a yellow suit.

She had asked me to sing at her funeral, and I had decided that in her honor, I would wear the brightest, prettiest thing in my closet and sing 'Celebrate Me Home' along with three other songs she had chosen. That particular song wasn't on the list, but it was perfect for her, and she couldn't very well say anything about it at that point!

Unfortunately, Auntie Alice passed away during the height of the COVID-19 pandemic, and I was not able to attend her funeral. I hope they buried her in her best party dress!

Paul is writing to the Philippian church from a jail cell in Rome, chained to a guard, hoping to be released, but very uncertain about his future. His hope is that Christ will be honored in his life or death, whichever this leads to. His desire is to be with Christ, but he also knows that the churches he has founded may still need him. Regardless, to live is Christ and to die is Christ, face to face.

When the word of Paul's execution came to his churches, I hope they were torn. Do we grieve our loss or celebrate his home-going to Jesus? Perhaps they had an Auntie Alice, who taught them they could do both at the same time.

Do you long to be with Jesus? I certainly do. To see him face to face will be my greatest joy. In the meantime, I will remain, honor Christ with courage and labor fruitfully. And when it is time: Celebrate me home!

Celebrate Me Home

Daywind Records: The Perrys Official Live Video.

Philippians 2:14-15/Matthew 5:14-16

My husband and I had to drive from Swift Current, Saskatchewan, to Bemidji, Minnesota, to pick up some parts for his business. At the time, it was cheaper to go get them than to ship them! We were away from home for 56 hours and drove for 24 of them.

So we spent quite a bit of time driving in the dark through sparsely populated country. It was January, and snowing, so there was heavy cloud cover, and it was dark out there. I could see the yard lights of farms and ranches sprinkled across the land, and because it was so dark, they caught my eye and held my attention. I could tell some of them were quite far away, and it got me thinking, just how far away could we see a light in the dark? It was not difficult to track a plane across the sky at night, just by its blinking lights. A pilot had estimated that at night, they could see the lights of another plane at about 35-50km away and city lights at about 230km distance.

Jesus told the crowds that we, his followers, are the light of the world that shines for God's glory by our good works, so don't cover them up!

Then Paul tells the Philippians that they are in a crooked and twisted generation, and they were to shine in the midst of it.

If ever there was a generation that could be called crooked, twisted and dark, we are in it! Our job is to shine in the middle of it. The light we bear should capture people's attention and draw them to the light. We have the greatest, most glorious light to share with them; Jesus!

Arise & Shine - New Wine Official Lyric Video

Other resources: Aviation.stackexchange.com, Nov 3, 2016, Question by Ron Beyer, Answer by pilot J W

Galatians 6:1-2/James 5:16-20

We are fortunate to have a dirt bike track just a few blocks from our home. During his last couple of years of high school, our son would often go over and ride his bike.

One day, he went over, and a couple of hours later, he staggered into the house bruised, battered, road-rashed and with a concussion. He had crashed. We're still not sure if he had lost consciousness. Some kind person packed him into their car, brought him home and made sure he got safely into the house. We don't know who they were, but we are so grateful.

What should we do when we see a brother or sister in Christ who has crashed? Perhaps their social media posts are inappropriate. Maybe there is an addiction, alcohol or anger problem, gossip, or any one of a list that is not honoring to the name of Christ they carry.

In Galatians 6:1-2, Paul tells us to go to them and gently restore them. Don't fall into temptation while you are with them. We help them bear the burden.

James tells us to confess our sins to one another and pray for one another so we can be healed.

He tells us that if we help bring back one who wanders from the truth, we have a part in saving them from spiritual death and help them in the process of Christ forgiving their sin.

We pack up the bruised, battered, and confused and carry them home to Jesus.

Redeemer, Savior, Friend – Keith Kitchen, Broomtree

1 Samuel 17:1-49

Did you notice how many characters there are in this chapter?! I kept having to go back and figure out who David was talking to now!

If you glance back at chapter 16, you get some context. David has already been anointed as the future king of Israel by Samuel, and he has already been in Saul's service as a musician and armor-bearer.

Verse 15 tells us David was going back and forth between serving Saul and home to help his father with the family's flock. David is often portrayed as a boy or young teen, but he was likely a grown man, though not old by any means. We usually think of David and Goliath—and maybe Saul—if we know the story. But there are plenty of dynamics in play, and David is bombarded with many voices.

In verses 1-10, we are introduced to Goliath of Gath, a Philistine of some impressive qualities. He's big. He's scary. He's loud. He's intimidating. Verse 11 tells us that Saul and the Israelite army were dismayed and afraid. Understandable!

First, we have Jesse, the voice of avoidance. "Take this food to your brothers and something for the commander, then get out of there and let me know how the boys are doing." Get in, keep your head down, get out.

David gets out to the battlefield to talk with his brothers and hears Goliath's challenge. He sees everyone flee from Goliath. In a conversation with other men in the army, he hears the voice of fear. "Have you seen the size of that guy?" Vs 24-25

His oldest brother, Eliab, overhears their conversation, and David hears the voice of discouragement. "What did you do with the sheep? You just came to see the battle, you presumptuous, evil-hearted kid." Vs 28

When the people bring David to Saul, because he's asking why no one will go fight Goliath, he hears the voice of doubt. "You can't fight him. You're a kid, and he's been fighting since he was your age." Vs 33

After explaining why, he was fully qualified to take on Goliath and confidently asserting that the Lord God of Israel would deliver Goliath into his hand, David heard the voice of resignation. Saul says, "Go, and the Lord be with you." Good luck. Here's my armor. Vs 37

David rejects the armor, gets 5 stones from the brook and goes out to meet Goliath. There, he hears the voice of disdain and defiance from Goliath. Vs 36 & 42-46

Not one of the voices took David's confidence. Everyone was looking horizontally at the big guy across the valley. At the young man who seemed so presumptuous, at the untested armor. David was looking vertically, to the Lord God of Israel, who could deliver him and Israel from God's enemy. Read verses 45-47 again.

Is there a battle you need to fight? Has God given you a job to do that others are trying to talk you out of? You can't do that, it's too big, you're too small, you should do something you can handle...

Whose voice are you going to listen to, and which direction are you looking?

Voice of Truth - Casting Crowns, New York Session

The Fruit of the Spirit

Galatians 5:16-26

My husband and I were in Florida for an ice cream course at the beginning of March a few years ago. Seasons are very different there. Where we live, you don't get fresh, ripe strawberries until mid-June. But there? The day before the course started, we went to a U-pick garden with acres of strawberries that were so ripe! They were bright red, incredibly juicy, and sweet. We snacked on lots and took some to our course to make the most fantastic fresh strawberry ice cream pops.

Almost everyone likes fruit. It's delicious, nourishing, and refreshing. The colors are vibrant. It's full of all kinds of vitamins and water that our bodies need.

A cool slice of watermelon on a hot day.

A fresh, crisp apple in the fall.

An orange is in peak season in January.

A splash of lemon in almost anything brightens flavors and can make a dish come to life.

In Galatians, Paul tells us that we, as believers, have fruit in our lives that is developed by the Holy Spirit. He starts verse 22 with 'But'. That usually means the verses before are the opposite of, or in contrast to, the verses we are about to read.

Paul calls them the works of the flesh, and they are listed in verses 19-21. He warns us that Christ-followers should not be doing these things. Those who have no inheritance in the kingdom of God.

The Fruit of the Spirit, however, is love, joy, peace, patience, kindness, goodness, faithfulness, gentleness and self-control. These become the characteristics by which believers are known. They show others that we are walking with the Holy Spirit.

Paul then reminds us not to be conceited, "I have more patience than that person." Or provoking one another. "If you are a Christian, you should have more self-control!" Or envying one another. "Why can't I have the kind of peace that person has?"

Notice that there are nine characteristics, but they are referred to as one 'fruit.' Even the verb 'is' rather than 'are' says that these are all linked together, so they need to grow together. The fruit on one tree will not all ripen on the same day, but they will all grow together and be at about the same stage of development. You don't see a tree with cherry blossoms and fully ripe cherries at the same time. If you have lots of love but no patience, or plenty of joy but no faith, there is a problem somewhere. With the Holy Spirit's help, you can weed out the problem and keep your fruit growing,

As we keep in step with the Spirit, our fruit will be attractive to those around us. And as we share it, we can nourish and refresh the people around us.

Hymn of the Holy Spirit - Pat Barrett

John 15:1-11

Our daughter is a sommelier. That's a fancy word for a person who is an expert in wine. While she was studying, I learned all kinds of things I never imagined I would know. For example, growing grapes in a vineyard is called viticulture. To my knowledge, no other fruit has its own word for growing it. The viticulture of a given vineyard gives the grapes grown their unique characteristics that shape the profile of the wine. Is the soil acidic, sandy, or volcanic? Which direction is the slope facing? Is the climate cool or hot, humid or dry? How are the vines pruned? When are the grapes harvested? If you know which characteristics all of the different variables give to wine, and you know where in the world those characteristics exist, you can, like our daughter, smell and taste a wine and tell what you are drinking and where it's from, even right down to the specific vineyard.

Jesus and his disciples finished their final meal together and started their walk to Gethsemane the evening before He was to be crucified (John 14:31). Knowing this was his last opportunity to pour Himself into his friends while He was still with them, He shared the most important things for them to remember.

As they walked along, perhaps they came upon a local vineyard. Or maybe He was thinking back to the wine they had shared around the communion table, and He says, "I am the true vine, My Father is the vinedresser" (vs.1).

Then in verse 5, He says, "I am the vine, you are the branches. Whoever abides in me and I in him, it is he that bears much fruit."

A branch gathers all it needs from the vine to produce its fruit. The fruit takes its characteristics from the vine. If the branch is not properly attached to the vine, the fruit will either not exist or will be poor.

As we are to grow the Fruit of the Spirit in our lives, we must stay securely connected to the Vine. Jesus calls that "abiding in him." It means we submit to God's pruning. We love Jesus and obey his commands. We have access to Jesus' joy that will fill us. We glorify God with our fruit and prove that we are Jesus' disciples (vs.8)

When people meet us, they should say, "I recognize the characteristics. This one grew in Jesus' vineyard."

Abide – Aaron Williams, Dwell Songs

1 Corinthians 13

Love

Love for God, love one another, love your neighbor, God is love. It is an overarching theme in the Bible, from beginning to end.

There is a reason Paul put it first in this Fruit of the Spirit list. All of the other fruits are characteristics of love.

Attributes of Love:

Joy (vs. 6): Love rejoices in truth.

Peace (vs. 11): There is a peace that comes with the maturity that love brings.

Patience (vs. 4 and 7): Love is patient. Love bears all things and endures all things.

Kindness (vs. 4-5): Love is kind, not rude or irritable.

Goodness (vs. 3 and 6): We can do good, but without love, it means nothing. Love does not rejoice in wrongdoing.

Faithfulness (vs. 3, 7, 12): Faith that moves mountains is nothing without love. Love believes and hopes all things. It looks forward to seeing Jesus face to face.

Gentleness (vs. 4-5): Love is not arrogant, does not boast.

Self-Control (vs. 4, 5, 11): It does not boast, does not insist on its own way, is not resentful. It behaves and thinks maturely, not like a child.

So now faith, hope, and love abide, but the greatest of these is love. Vs 13

The Love of God – Guy Penrod, Blessed Assurance

Psalm 4

Joy

One of my pastors did a sermon on "The Joy of the Lord is Our Strength." It was good, but I went to his office later that week and told him I had a problem with Sunday's message. He was a bit taken aback because I was normally on board with what he was preaching.

I told him that drawing on the joy God gives us is good. I understand the link between joy and strength. I basically told him his sermon was right on point.

And then I said, "What do you do when you have lost your joy?"

By the end of our talk, he thought he should maybe do a follow-up sermon: "The Joy of the Lord is Our Strength: The Prequel."

Let's see where the Lord gives us our joy.

Psalm 51:12: Restore to me the joy of your salvation. Joy comes in Jesus' salvation of us.

Zephaniah 3:17: He (God) will rejoice over you with gladness… He will exalt over you with singing. Imagining the God of heaven rejoicing and singing over me? It's humbling, but it gives me such joy.

Psalm 16:11: There is fullness of joy in God's presence.

Psalm 119:111: God's Word brings joy to our hearts.

1 Thessalonians 2:19-20: The people of God and those we have nurtured in their faith.

1 Thessalonians 4:16-17 For the Lord himself shall descend from heaven with a cry of command, with the voice of the archangel and with the sound of the trumpet of God. And the dead in Christ will rise first. Then we who are alive, who are left, will be caught up together with them in the clouds to meet the Lord in the air, and so we will always be with the Lord! (Mic drop!)

This is just the tip of the iceberg; there are many more verses about joy in the Bible. Let me leave you with this thought today: There is great joy in our hope of heaven.

Endless Hallelujah – Matt Redman, 10,000 Reasons

Philippians 4

Peace

The Canadian Mental Health Association has an article titled "Mental Health Facts in Canada 2024." According to this article:

- Approximately 20% of Canadian youth are affected by a mental illness or disorder.
- Anxiety disorders affect 4.6% of the population.
- By age 40, about 50% of the population will have or have had a mental illness.
- The economic cost of mental illnesses to the Canadian healthcare and social support system was projected as $79.9 billion for 2021.

Peace is something our world so desperately needs. Whether it is a mental illness, a broken or anxious heart, or the circumstances we are in, we long for peace. Just let everything be calm, and maybe this panic/anxiety/depression will go away.

It's not that easy. Dragging yourself out of depression is nearly impossible. Calming a panic attack can take hours and is exhausting. A sunny day at the lake isn't going to solve the underlying problem.

Yet, as believers, we are to have peace as one of the signatures of our relationship with Jesus. Where do we find it? How do we get it?

Job 38: Know, without a doubt, that God is in control. Of everything. From creation to the end of time. He is sovereign, and

He loves us. That combination of characteristics of God should give us great confidence in Him.

Proverbs 3:5-6: "Trust in the Lord with all your heart and do not lean on your own understanding. In all your ways acknowledge Him, and He will make your paths straight." When you are tangled in worry or fear, go to God's Word. Trust Him, not your own thoughts. Recognize that He is all-knowing and all-wise, and He alone can straighten out your thoughts.

John 14:25-27: Jesus promises that the Holy Spirit will be sent by His Father after He is gone. It's not the same kind of peace that the world says it can give us, so we can trust Him.

Philippians 4:6-8 "The peace of God, which surpasses all understanding, will guard your hearts and minds in Christ Jesus."

Remember that the Lord is near. Bring your anxieties, fears, worries, and pain to God. It's God's peace, and He will guard your mind and heart in Christ Jesus. And, as always, we have a part in it as well. Verse 8: Determine to think about things that are:

True
Honorable
Just
Pure
Lovely
Commendable
Excellent
Praiseworthy

It is hard when you are in the middle of everything that is causing your fears, but as with all the Fruit of the Spirit, it starts small and grows.

Wonderful Peace – Fairhope – Lyrics on the next page.

Wonderful Peace

Fairhope

Far away in the depths of my spirit tonight
Rolls a melody sweeter than psalm
In celestial strains it unceasingly falls
O'er my soul like an infinite calm

Refrain:
Peace! Peace! Wonderful peace
Coming down from the Father above
Sweep over my spirit forever, I pray
In fathomless billows of love

What a treasure have I in this wonderful peace
Buried deep in the heart of the soul
So secure that no power can mine it away
While the years of eternity roll

I am resting tonight in this wonderful peace
Resting sweetly in Jesus' control
For I'm kept from all danger by night and by day
And his glory is flooding my soul.

And me-thinks when I rise to that City of peace
Where the Author of peace I shall see
That one strain of song which the ransomed will sing
In that heavenly kingdom will be

By Warren D. Cornell and W. George Cooper
Copyright 1889, Warren D. Cornell and W. George Cooper

Psalm 27: 1-14

Patience

Television has not helped us in our expectations. In an hour, you can put out a wildfire, cure cancer, subvert an international crime ring, renovate your house, and find your soulmate. Or in a half hour, you should be able to solve your relationship problems and laugh about it while you do it.

It has not helped us be patient at all.

I would say that many Christians have a love-hate relationship with growing patience in their lives. They want to be patient; they know it's important. But they don't want to deal with what they instinctively know they will have to, to develop it.

"If I pray for patience, God's going to put me in a situation that requires it. And I don't have the patience for that!"

Let's look at the way that God teaches us to be patient.

First, He gives us examples of patience in Himself. In 1 Timothy 1:15-16, Paul tells us that Christ's perfect patience is displayed in saving and showing mercy to the worst of sinners.

Second, He shows us patience with other people in the Bible. Think of Jacob, working seven years to marry Rachel, only to find he has been tricked into marrying Leah and has to work seven more years to have Rachel. (Genesis 29:9-29)

Third, Psalm 40:1 Patience and perseverance are often linked. Perseverance without patience can look like dogged determination, or it can look like stubbornness or a selfish demand to have things done my way. When perseverance is tempered with patience, we see that others may need time to understand what I am saying or doing. Or as we persist in praying for and sharing with that person we love who isn't a believer, but we have to patiently wait for God to do His work in their lives.

Romans 12:12 is the fourth way we are taught patience by God. We are to be "patient in tribulation."

There are people in our world who understand what tribulation is far better than I do. And they learn patience in those things far more quickly than I do. But we all have things that we need to wait for that are troubling. A relationship that needs to be restored. A boss who seems to be neglecting what you need to do your job well. A fellow believer who will not obey the scripture. This is patience that stays calm in the face of things that could cause you to be annoyed and angry. It requires understanding that you cannot control your circumstances, but you can control how you react to your circumstances.

As with all of these Fruit of the Spirit, you have an active part in growing patience along with the Holy Spirit. Make the choice to be patient in little things, and you will gradually build patience for the big things.

Patience - The Music Machine

Yes, I Will – Vertical Worship, Bright Faith, Bold Future.

Titus 3:1-11

Goodness

As I began to think through goodness, I realized that it is a very abstract thing. What is the essence of goodness? The outward actions of goodness show up in kindness and other Fruits of the Spirit, but what does it mean to be good?

According to Webster's dictionary, goodness is "the quality of being good or the state of being good." Not helpful.

Then I checked the definition of "good." It's extensive. The two primary categories of "good" are:

Of a favorable character or tendency

Virtuous, Right, Commendable

So, goodness is a state of favorable character and tendency and a state of being virtuous, right, and commendable.

Paul, in his letters to Titus, is giving him instructions on how to lead and teach the church he has been charged with. In verse 1 of Chapter 3, he says, "Remind them... to be ready for every good work." Read through the chapter again and make a chart of what Paul says are good works and what are not. I'll get you started!

Good Works	Not Good Works
1. Submission to Rulers	1. Speaking Evil

I think we can conclude that good works come from a good character.

Verses 4-7 tell us about how to develop a good character.

Verse 4: Goodness is part of Jesus' character.

Verse 5: Because Jesus is good, He saved us. But He didn't save us because of the good things we have done, even in righteousness. He saved us because of His mercy. Then the Holy Spirit washes us and makes us new.

Verse 6: Jesus didn't hold back. He gave us mercy and the Holy Spirit abundantly.

Verse 7: We are justified by Jesus' grace and know we have a place with Him for eternity.

In verse 8, Paul tells us that those who have experienced verses 4-7 should devote themselves to good works because they are excellent and profitable for the people around us.

A-ha moment! Our goodness is not for us. It's for others!

Jesus said, "Let your light shine before men, that they may see your good works, and glorify your Father who is in heaven." (Matthew 5:16)

The Holy Spirit regenerates us and makes our character good, so when others see us, they are attracted to Jesus, and then they will also glorify God!

Goodness goes from abstract to concrete.

Are you letting your fruit of goodness attract others to Jesus? Ask the Holy Spirit to show you places today where you can be good.

How Good is He – Vertical Worship, Song Sessions.

Micah 6:6-8

Kindness

The Hebrew word for kindness is "khesed." It starts with a sound we don't make in English unless we have a cold and are trying to clear unwanted stuff from our throats. It is used 248 times in the Scriptures and translated into English several different ways.

Sarah Fisher, in her article, says: "But this word, khesed, isn't just kindness, it's literally kindness wrapped in love, and so it's often translated as lovingkindness... although some translations use mercy, loyal love, or loving devotion. This expression of lovingkindness makes sense, because every time you are expressing kindness, you are also expressing love... (Kindness is love in action). You cannot separate kindness and love; they are a package deal."

Our passage in Micah asks, "With what shall I come before the Lord?" All the sacrifices mean little to Him. You can offer what you have or what is impossible for you to acquire. But what does God require of you?

To do justice

To love kindness

To walk humbly with Him

Our actions of kindness toward others are a sacrifice that pleases God. And it is something He requires of us. Whether it is forgiving someone who has wronged us, helping the poor, caring for the lonely, binding a wound, or helping mend a broken heart, they are all ways of showing God's loving kindness through our actions.

Step out of your comfort zone today. Do something extravagantly kind for someone you would not normally do it for. The harder part might be to tell that person that they are deeply loved by God and, therefore, by you as well.

Kindness – Steven Curtis Chapman, Official Lyric Video

Other Resources: Sarah E. Fisher, "Speaking of Kindness" (July 14, 2024) at www.hebrewwordlessons.com.

Hebrews 11

Faithfulness

I am not a very sporty person. The point of most sports is lost on me, but I certainly respect the physical ability, dedication, stamina, and mental sharpness it requires to be exceptional at something. Most players of a given sport will not be remembered beyond when they play with a team, but the truly special are often inducted into their "Hall of Fame." Their display will have pictures, some background stories, and artifacts like their uniforms or equipment. Their statistics and all of the awards they have won will be listed. Often, even a trophy or two will be displayed.

When I think of faithfulness, the first thing that comes to mind is God's "Hall of Faith." Here you can find examples of people who were faithful to God, using His standards. From Abel to Samuel and the prophets, God tells us the whys' and how's of faithfulness and reminds us that this list is not complete. There are always more faithful ones to add.

Verses 35-38

Faithfulness is the one Fruit of the Spirit that has more to do with our relationship with God than with other people.

It is helpful that we have a very clear definition of faith in Hebrews 11:1: "Now faith is the assurance of things hoped for, the conviction of things not seen."

Faith is believing what the Word of God says and standing firmly on that belief, from the creation of the universe by God's word (v.3) to the promise of a heavenly home (v.15-16).

Faith is acting in obedience to what you know God has told you. The pattern is repeated over and over in this chapter: "By faith, this person did this when God told them to do it."

The test was always difficult, like building an ark when it had never rained (v.7), or impossible, like conceiving a baby in your nineties when your husband is also "as good as dead" (v.11-12).

Faith is knowing that, regardless of the hardship you face now, God has made promises of eternity. My trophies are there, not here, and I will have to wait for them. The Hall of Faith-ers are still waiting for their rewards. Verses 39-40 tell us that all of us will receive our rewards for our faithfulness when we are together in heaven.

So, in short, faithfulness is about believing and trusting what God tells us, even though we can't see Him or the end result. It's about obedience and knowing, without wavering, that He has an eternal home and rewards ready for us when it's time.

I may not be a Hall of Faith-er, but I sure want to be on the team. As I grow and learn, maybe I can score a few points to add to my stats and have a trophy or two to lay at Jesus' feet.

Stand in Faith – Danny Gokey, Official Lyric Video

James 3:13-18

Gentleness

One of the first things we start to teach our children is gentleness.

Babies don't have good motor skills. Arms and legs flail around. Tiny fingers with sharp fingernails grasp and scratch, and a big head on a wobbly neck needs support, or it will hit your nose and make you cry!

When babies start to physically interact with their surroundings, we start teaching them to be gentle. We'll take their hand and show them how to gently touch a person's face. When they are introduced to a kitten or puppy, we teach them how to pet them gently and calmly. We show them how to hold delicate things like a flower or jewelry with care and gentleness.

Then we praise them until gentleness becomes a natural part of how they handle things around them.

Have you ever been around a child who has not been taught gentleness? Or perhaps for one reason or another, hasn't been able to learn it? It is not a pleasant experience.

For Christ followers, gentleness is a characteristic by which we should be recognized. It is one of our Holy Spirit-grown fruits.

Obviously, gentleness is not just physical. It is part of how we think, speak and behave. It comes from our heart and is an indication of how we are growing and maturing in our relationships with Jesus and others.

James tells us that we should conduct ourselves with meekness and wisdom that comes from above. Wisdom from above is wisdom from God, which we find in our Bibles. This wisdom from above is pure, peaceable, gentle, open to reason, full of mercy and good fruit, impartial and sincere. (v. 17-18)

The opposite is laid out in verses 14-15. Bitter jealousy, selfish ambition, boasting, and lying are all signs of the immature, earthly, and unspiritual. And, more so, can be demonic! They lead to disorder and vile practices.

If the Holy Spirit is prompting your heart to be more gentle, it's time to start learning from mature believers who display gentleness. Notice how they speak and interact with people. How do they handle a person who disagrees with them? Do they demand that people listen to them or calmly discuss things? How do they show graciousness to people around them? Let them take your hand and show you how to be gentle with the weak and delicate.

Your gentleness will show others that you are a fruit-growing, maturing believer in Jesus.

Gentle Like Jesus – Sovereign Grace Music

1 Corinthians 10

Self-Control

When we talked about faithfulness, we mentioned that it is the fruit that is about our relationship with God. Well, self-control is the one most closely connected to our personal life.

There are several ways to approach the fruit of self-control. We could discuss our spiritual habits. We could look at it through how the other fruits are displayed in your life. We could approach it from the direction of maturity and growth.

Today, we are going to talk about self-control when temptation comes along. Think for a few moments about the things you are easily tempted by. I'm not talking about your last run-in with a chocolate cake (unless gluttony is a problem!) or hitting your snooze button an extra time on the occasional morning. What are the things you know are ungodly that you struggle letting go of? What do you have to come to Jesus with and repent of over and over again? What comes along and fouls up your relationships with people because you can't seem to overcome it?

Let's take a look at what Paul tells the Corinthians about self-control in the face of temptation.

In verse 6, Paul says, "These things took place as an example for us." Dive into the Word. When a story shows up where people didn't deal well with temptation, consider it an example of what not to do.

Be aware. Even though the Israelites were all under the same cloud of God, being led by the same cloud in the desert, eating the same food, having the same experiences, God was not pleased with most of them. Temptation overthrew them in the desert. Know what your pitfalls are so you can see them coming. (v. 1-6 and 7-10)

Stand firm and take heed. Even the strongest believers can fall. (v. 12) Pay attention. Remember, even a strong person can be led from being faithful. Pay attention to the warnings in the Bible and from other godly people.

Don't think you are alone. (v. 13a) Guaranteed, there is someone around you who has the same struggle.

Trust God. He will not let you face a situation that He knows you will fail at. But He will sometimes let you come face to face with something He knows you will be tempted by. It helps you grow in Him and be stronger. (v. 13b)

God will always provide a way of escape (v. 13c). Now, keep in mind that God will provide a way of escape, but you have to take it. We still have free will. We can duck out the side door, or we can walk right into a situation we know we shouldn't be in.

When all else fails, turn around and run! (v. 14) You can't flee from something if you are trying to run backwards! Turn around and get your eyes off of what is tempting you, then get moving as fast and far away as possible!

Each step requires you to use your self-control and self-discipline.

Paul finishes his list of the Fruit of the Spirit with Galatians 5:24:

"Those who belong to Christ Jesus have crucified the flesh with its passions and desires."

Our old man is dead. We are new creations in Christ, and He is our Lord now. Keep your fruit growing!

Lord, I Need You – Matt Maher, All the People Said Amen, 2013

Psalm 119:1-16

Did you know...

Purple garage doors are illegal in Kanata, Ontario.

If your parrot talks too loudly, you could be fined $100 in Oak Bay, BC. Removing your feet from bicycle pedals is illegal in Ottawa, Ontario.

In Alberta, when you are released from prison, the government is still required to give you a handgun, bullets, and a horse. (I'm pretty sure they don't do this anymore!)

You can, however, be fined for painting a wooden ladder.

In Dartmouth, Nova Scotia, it's illegal to have a chipped or cracked bathtub.

And don't even get me started on some goofy laws in the USA!!

At the end of the Fruit of the Spirit list, Paul adds, "Against such things, there is no law." You would be hard-pressed anywhere in the world to find a law against being kind, patient, joyful, or gentle. There simply is no need for such a thing.

Jesus reminds us in Matthew 22:36-40 that the two most important laws in God's Word are to "Love the Lord your God with all your heart, soul, mind, and strength and to love your neighbor as yourself." If you do those two things, the Fruit of the Spirit will not only grow in your life, but you'll have people around you to put them into action!

Galatians 5:25 says, "If we live by the Spirit, let us also keep in step with the Spirit." We don't want to run ahead or lag behind.

Walking in the laws of the Lord seems to be a good way to practice. Learn to love the instructions given in the Word. Keep growing and sharing the Fruit of the Spirit!

Psalm 119 is all about God's Word. In just the first few verses, there are so many blessings to staying in step with the Spirit by following God's Word.

Verse 1: If you walk in the law of the Lord, you will be blameless.

Verse 2: If you seek Him, you will be blessed.

Verse 5: Your ways will be steadfast.

Verse 9: Your way will be kept pure by guarding it with God's Word.

Verse 10: By seeking the Lord with your whole heart, you will not wander.

Verse 11: God's Word in your heart will keep you from sin.

Verse 14: You can delight in the testimonies of God's Word.

There are 160 more verses to discover and learn from in Psalm 119!

So, keep your fruit growing.

Stay connected to your Vine, Jesus.

Get into God's Word and obey it.

Keep in step with the Holy Spirit.

Lord, I Have Made Thy Word My Choice – Issac Watts, Saint Michael's Singers

Other Resources: Kahane Law Office, April 4, 2018, Wacky Wednesday: Wacky Laws Across the Provinces.

Psalm 136

Perhaps you picked up on the key phrase in this psalm? Now go back and read it again, but skip all of the 'For His steadfast love endures forever's.

> Give thanks to the Lord, for He is good
>
> Give thanks to the God of gods
>
> Give thanks to the Lord of lords

The whole psalm is about giving thanks to God for who he is and what he has done. Creation, saving Israel from Egypt, moving them to their own land, remembering them when they were in exile and taking care of their needs.

Why did God do all of these things? Because His steadfast love endures forever.

This steadfast love is the same khesed love we have talked about that is also translated as lovingkindness, mercy, and gracious love. Because of this deep, merciful love for his people, God protected, led, provided for and disciplined them. He does the same for us.

Remember and be thankful for God's enduring, steadfast love. It is solid through every trial, every battle and every exile we must walk through. And be thankful because it is the same love that provides all our needs, rescues us and settles us in a good place. He loves us so deeply that he will do whatever it takes to save us.

C.S. Lewis, in his book, Mere Christianity, says;

"The great thing to remember is that, though our failings come and go, His love for us does not. It is not wearied by our sins, or our indifference; and therefore, it is quite relentless in its determination that we shall be cured of those sins at whatever cost to us, at whatever cost to him."

Oh, How He Loves You and Me – George Beverley Shea, The Ultimate Collection

Other resources: C.S. Lewis, Mere Christianity, Scribner Paper Fiction, 1952

Isaiah 41:8-10/Revelation 21:1-7

July 1, 2011, was a sunny, beautiful summer day. It was Canada Day, so there were lots of travelers heading out on their holidays, including my friends, Steve and Hilda. Steve was an upholsterer in our community, and Hilda was my hairdresser. They had lived in Swift Current for a long time and were known in some capacity by almost everyone.

They were anticipating a two-week vacation in the Rocky Mountains, and that morning, they packed up their motorcycle and headed west.

By 1 pm that day, all of the prayer chains in town were notified, and everyone was praying. Near Webb, about 20 minutes from home, their motorcycle had crashed into the right-hand ditch. No one knew exactly what had happened to cause it. Steve and Hilda were both alive, but not in good condition. Steve had broken vertebrae and ribs, and one knee that was torn to pieces inside. Hilda was severely injured with breaks to her vertebrae and ribs as well, and several other bones, and a serious brain injury. She was in a coma, and the chance of her surviving was questionable.

The team the RCMP sent out to investigate the accident was the one usually reserved for events that had been fatal, so they likely should not have even survived.

Hilda was airlifted to a hospital in Saskatoon, and Steve was taken to the same hospital by ambulance to begin the long process of healing.

One way or another, I knew Hilda would be okay. While praying for her one day, the Lord allowed me to see her hospital room, and there the Holy Spirit was hovering over her bed, protecting and covering her. The Spirit was right there, ready to take her to heaven if the Father so said, or to heal her for more service here. I peppered our pastor with questions about just what her room looked like: "Where was the window? What direction was the bed facing? What machines was she attached to?" And his description lined up with what I had seen!

Hilda did recover, with a long road of healing behind and ahead of her. She has had vision, speech, memory and mobility challenges. But this dear sister in the Lord is a walking testimony to God's faithfulness. She is never without a smile, a hug and an encouraging word. The day she was able to play piano at a local restaurant was a celebration for everyone who knew her, whether they could attend or not. She and Steve are more in love than they ever have been, and she loves the Lord and the people around her with a passion that overflows.

When I asked her if she had a couple of verses that had sustained her through everything, she gave me these:

Isaiah 41:10: "Do not fear, for I am with you. Do not be dismayed, for I am your God. I will strengthen you; I will uphold you with my righteous right hand."

Revelation 21:4: "I will wipe every tear from your eyes. There will be no more death or crying or pain, for the old order has passed away."

Hilda has learned that her physical disabilities mean nothing in the light of God's strength, goodness and promises. And there will be a day when Jesus will remove it all, and she will be perfect!

Day by Day – Songs and Everlasting Joy, Carolina Sandell Berg

Joshua 22

Have you ever done something for good, and the people around you completely misunderstood your motivation? They thought you were doing it out of rebellion or sinfulness? I have. It's very easy to get defensive, hurt and angry.

In this case, Joshua sent the tribes home after a long series of battles to conquer the promised land. The tribes of Reuben, Gad and Manasseh had land assigned to them to the east of the Jordan River. They realized that they were separated by this barrier from the rest of the nation, so they built a big altar to remind the westerners that they were all one family.

The western tribes saw the altar and assumed it was for sacrificing, but God had said they were only to sacrifice on the altar at the Tabernacle. They gathered for a civil war because they had made assumptions and not asked the questions! Someone finally had the wherewithal to send the elders over to find out what was going on. Once the questions were asked and the answers given, Phineas, the priest said, "Today we know the Lord is in our midst, because you have not committed a breach of faith against the Lord."

When believers can have honest discussions about what is happening in and around us, it can dissipate so much conflict. Often, we can learn that what we thought was a major problem was a misunderstanding of a person's actions. But we have to take the time to ask questions and listen to the other person's heartfelt answers.

When we can resolve a potential conflict, we know that 'the Lord is in our midst!'

God wants us to be unified, and when we are, He is right there with us.

Build Your Kingdom Here – Rend Collective

Psalm 66

When I was in high school, we had a very talented pianist in our church. When she played 'How Great Thou Art', each verse was slower, bigger and fancier than the last one. This dear sister used the entire piano, and playing that song was an act of worship for her. The song was an event when she was playing, and the congregation came to the throne along with her! Hearts and voices lifted in corporate worship to praise God for all He had done. It was wonderful!

Psalm 66 praises God with joy! It talks about His glory, power and His amazing miracles. He sustains our lives, tests and disciplines us and then brings us to a place of abundance, so we can respond to Him and then invite others to join us.

Three times, the psalmist uses the term 'Selah'. The sense of this term is to take a moment, pause, and reflect on what has just been said or sung. Allow the truth of it to sink into your heart and then respond to God with fuller understanding.

Praising God needs to be done with both your heart and your head! When the Samaritan woman asked Jesus where the appropriate place to worship was, he responded that the physical location is not as important as worshipping in spirit and in truth, heart and head. John 4:19-24

There are times when we sing worship songs with joyful abandon, and there are times to take a moment of quietness to humble ourselves before God's greatness, majesty and holiness. Selah

How Great Thou Art – Paul Hankinson Covers, Peaceful Piano Version

How Great Thou Art

Carl Boberg, Swedish Folk Song, 1885

Oh Lord, My God
When I, in awesome wonder
Consider all the worlds Thy hands have made
I see the stars, I hear the rolling thunder
Thy power throughout the world is displayed.

Refrain:
Then sings my soul,
My Savior, God, to Thee
How great Thou art
How great Thou art

When through the woods and forest glades I wander
And hear the birds sing sweetly in the trees
When I look down from lofty mountain grandeur
And hear the brook and feel the gentle breeze

And when I think that God, his Son, not sparing
Sent him to die, I scarce can take it in
That on the cross, my burden gladly bearing
He bled and died to take away my sin

When Christ shall come, with shout of acclamation
To take me home, what joy shall fill my heart
Then I shall bow, in humble adoration
And there proclaim, "My God, how great Thou art!"

Psalm 8

At worship practice one evening, we were doing a final run-through at the end. We usually read the scripture reading at that time to determine when the next intro should start, and that week it happened to be Psalm 8. Now, our team tends to be a bit older, even though we play very contemporary music (and we do it fairly well!), so when the worship leader said, "Oh Lord, our Lord, how majestic is your name in all the earth!" we all automatically started singing Michael W. Smith's version of the song. You can't help yourself—the words and rhythmic melody are deeply ingrained in everyone who was a Christian in the 80's.

The psalm doesn't stop there, of course. Verse 2 is very interesting. It seems not quite go with the rest of the verses, so there must be a reason.

"Out of the mouths of babies and infants, you have established strength because of your foes, to still the enemy and the avenger."

What does that even mean? Babies and infants are weak and powerless. How can God use that against His enemies?

I think it is a beautiful picture of how God uses the weakest, the smallest person or thing to accomplish His purposes. Think of Moses's staff. It was just a branch until God used it as a tool of faith in Moses' hand. (Exodus 14:15-18)

Or one kid in a crowd willingly hands his lunch to Jesus, and it feeds thousands (John 6:1-13)

Or by offering Jesus a drink of water, a woman with a poor reputation hears the gospel, and many are saved in her city. (John 4:5-30)

The psalmist goes on to ask, "And the Creator, why would ever think of humankind?" Creation seems so vast, so powerful, so incredible, and then there is me. I am about as helpful as a baby against a whole army... Hmmm, interesting.

Still, God gave us dominion over His creation here on earth and entrusted us with its care. Whether you think we have done a great or poor job of it, the fact that God would trust us with it is pretty amazing.

We can also look at this psalm in a messianic sense. While Jesus was here with us on earth, He willingly set aside some of His glory and power to be like us, a little lower than the angels. Because of this, He was able to redeem us by His death on the cross and is seated at the right hand of His Father, where He is again over all things. Yet He intercedes for us. (Philippians 2:5-11, Romans 8:34)

Oh Lord, Our Lord, how majestic is your name in all the earth!

How Majestic is Your Name - Sandi Patti, Michael W. Smith

Romans 8:31-39

There are a couple of things to note about this passage that help to make more sense of the verses.

First of all, it starts with a question. "What then shall we say to these things?"

All of Romans 8 is packed with doctrine:

Living in the Spirit, not according to the law of the flesh
The hope of resurrection
Who we are when we are led by the Spirit
The hope of heaven
Conforming to Christ-likeness
This chapter touches on so much doctrine that helps us walk out our relationship with Jesus while we are here.

All of those doctrines are 'these things.' So, verses 31-39 are a response to the richness of what God is doing in our lives through Jesus Christ!

The second mental note to make when you read this passage is to whom it is written. The church in Rome was in the middle of the persecution fire. They lived in a city where Caesar was enthroned and often expected to be worshipped. They were persecuted, hunted, murdered, and their lives could be destroyed at a word. When we read this passage in the comfort of our homes and the security of our church congregation, we don't really grasp the intensity of what Paul is writing.

But for these Roman Christians, tribulation, distress, persecution, famine, nakedness, danger and sword were very real possibilities every day.

Verse 36 is quoted from Psalm 44:22, which talks about Israel being punished by other nations, feeling like they were just a flock of sheep, good for nothing but to be killed and eaten. What a hopeless feeling. It would be understandable to feel like you had been abandoned by the God you had given your life to, and very well might have to give your life for.

But Paul reminds them that even though they face what seems like the impossible every day, they will be conquerors in it all if they just cling to the One who loves them.

Absolutely nothing can separate us from the Love of God in Jesus Christ our Lord!

The Promise – The Martins, Above It All

Ephesians 2:18-22/1 Peter 2:11-12

When I was a child, I always felt like I was weird. I never felt like I really belonged anywhere. I was different than the kids at school. They were confident and loud; I was shy and quiet. Most of them had siblings closer in age; I was the older sister with one brother almost 8 years younger, and I had grown up around adults. They seemed to know all the schoolyard games and sports things; I read everything I could get my hands on, and my favorite place was the library. I was different enough to get picked on and bullied regularly.

In Sunday School and church clubs, because of the reading I did, I always knew the answers to things the other kids were bored with, or it was new information to them. I didn't fit there either.

Even at home, there were times I felt very alone. I became a Christian when I was 4, and though Mom and Dad nurtured that as best they could, they didn't become Christians until I was 9. So the presence of the Holy Spirit in my life just made me think differently sometimes.

Then, one Sunday morning when I was about 12, I sat in church, and the pastor spoke on 1 Peter 2:11 &12. I don't remember what the last half of the sermon was about (though I can surmise that from the passage), but I remember so clearly how he explained what 'strangers and pilgrims' meant in this verse. And he finished that part of his sermon with something like, "So if you feel like you don't belong here, that's good, because you don't! Your home is in heaven, and when you get there, then you will know what it feels like to really be home!"

Flashing lightbulbs, bells, angels singing "Hallelujah!" All of those things happened in my brain all at once! I am not supposed to fit in here! In fact, if I do, there is something wrong in my spiritual walk.

I'm not home yet. Some days I still feel like I'm the weird one. Sometimes I still feel like I just don't quite fit in, even in my church family. But one day I'll be home! I'll see Jesus face to face, and he will show me what it means to feel like I belong!

Where I Belong – Building 429

Psalm 9

Verse 7: "The Lord sits enthroned forever; He has established His throne for justice, And He judges the world with righteousness; He judges the people with uprightness." We have a tendency in our churches to avoid talking about God as a righteous judge who has enemies He will destroy. We like to think about God as loving, not willing that any would perish. How many times in a scripture reading during a worship service does the person read the "pleasant" parts of a psalm and skip over the rest because it is too—well, too graphic?

We like to sing songs about Him making a way for sinners and as the King on the throne forever. We sing songs about God being holy, righteous and victorious, but we don't like to think about the other side of the coin. If God is holy, He cannot, because of His holiness, allow unholiness in His presence. If God is righteous, he cannot allow sin to go unpunished. If God is victorious, there are enemies He must be victorious over.

David, of all the psalmists, seems to have the most thorough understanding of these things. Many of his psalms speak of the enemies of God and His people being destroyed and perishing. He has no problem calling the wicked, evildoers, and enemies exactly what they are and telling about what will happen to them.

David also gives a very clear picture of God as the stronghold for the oppressed, vs 9, the avenger of blood from the afflicted, vs 12 and the one who lifts us from the gates of death

Verse 17 says, "The wicked shall return to Sheol, all the nations that forget God."

We must remember and accept that there are people and nations who are God's enemies, and there is a place reserved for them. If they did not receive their punishment in their lifetime, they will receive it at the end of time at God's judgment throne.

Verses 19 and 20 ask the Lord to arise! "Do not let man prevail; let the nations be judged before you! Put them in fear, O Lord! Let the nations know they are but men!"

Are we, as a church, presenting a weak gospel because we fail to tell people that if they are not coming to Him, they are His enemy? There are only two options. You fear God and come to Him in humility, repent, and obey OR you are His enemy, and you will see the judgment of a holy God.

Adore and Tremble – Daniel Renstrom

Psalm 10

In our time in Psalm 9, we talked about God's judgment on His enemies and the wicked. Psalm 10 is all about the characteristics of the wicked.

David starts by asking God Why He doesn't seem to be close and present when there is trouble for the poor, the innocent, the helpless, and the afflicted.

There are many characteristics here of the wicked:

Verse 2: He is arrogant and devious.

Verse 3: He is boastful, greedy.

Verse 4: There is pride on his face.

Verse 5: His ways seem to prosper (but we know how that turns out!); he ignores the judgment of God.

Verse 7: His mouth spits cursing, deceit, oppression, mischief, and iniquity.

Verse 8: He lurks in hiding to ambush the innocent.

Verse 9: He entraps the poor for his own gain.

What I find most interesting, though, is what the wicked decides and says about God.

Verse 3 says He renounces the Lord.

Verse 4 says All his thoughts are, 'There is no God."

Verse 6 says, in his heart, he believes he is immovable and that nothing can stop him.

Verse 11 says, He thinks God has forgotten the people who are unjustly treated. He isn't even looking, and He'll never see it. I can get away with anything.

In verse 13, he says to God, "You won't judge me."

Did you notice that the first thing he decides is that there is no God, but then spends the rest of his thoughts on convincing himself how God will not act, defend, see or judge? Deep inside, he knows that God is real and just.

The best verse in this psalm is verse 14!!

"But you <u>do</u> see, for you note mischief and vexation, that you may take it into your own hands."

God sees it all. He's taking notes, and He <u>will</u> take justice into His own hands. He <u>will</u> take down the evildoers, and He <u>will</u> judge wickedness until it is all cleaned out (v. 15).

Yet God hears the cries of the afflicted, the fatherless, the oppressed, and the helpless. He will strengthen them, and He promises justice.

God is present, even when we look around us and say, "Where is He? Why won't He do something?" For now, we trust Him, we rely on Him, we cry to Him, and we believe Him.

Lord of All – Kristian Stanfill

Sheep and Shepherds

Genesis 4:1-16

The first significant mention of a sheep in the Bible is in Genesis, when Cain and Abel are bringing their offerings to the Lord. Cain brought Fruit of the ground, so grain or vegetables, something like that. Abel brought the firstborn of his flock. God accepted Abel's lamb, but rejected Cain's grain.

Why?

It is a matter of the heart. When God rejected Cain's offering, his first response was anger, and apparently, he wasn't good at hiding it as his face fell.

God says to Cain, (my paraphrase) "What is your problem? If you do well, will you not be accepted?"

Cain's life was characterized by anger, violence, defensiveness, belligerence and maybe a little whining. God reminds him that if "he does not do well, sin is crouching at the door and its desire is for you. You need to rule over it."

God tells Cain that just sacrificing whatever you have will not keep you from sin. You have to actively be aware of your heart and align it with God's expectations. Don't give sin and temptation a foothold, or they will consume you.

Cain did not take the warning. Abel dies, and God and Cain deal with the consequences.

The saddest part of this passage, to me, is not that Abel is murdered or Cain is punished. It is verse 16 where it says, "Cain went away from the presence of the Lord." The implication is that Cain made a decision to walk away rather than repent and do well.

When sin is crouching at the door, and God is asking me to control it, and use some self-control, do I sometimes open the door and welcome it in? Or do I place myself under the will of Almighty God who loves me, wants to accept me and gave His Son on the cross to make that possible?

Acceptable to You - Calvin Institute of Christian Worship - July 24, 2020

Genesis 48:15-16/Genesis 49:22-26/Psalm 61

In these passages, we see Jacob, now known as Israel, blessing Joseph's two sons, Ephraim and Manasseh, and then blessing Joseph. This is the first time in the scriptures that we see anyone referring to God as their Shepherd.

Jacob's life had been full of deceit and trouble.

As a young man, he had taken his older brother's birthright and deceitfully taken Esau's blessing when Isaac was intending to give it to the elder son. His mom helped him, so we know where the sneaky genetics came from!

It was Jacob who wrestled with God, which would have been a Theophany. A Theophany is a physical appearance of Jesus Christ in the Old Testament. This was when his name was changed from Jacob to Israel.

It was Jacob who showed such favoritism to Joseph that Joseph's brothers sold him into slavery and told Jacob an animal had killed him.

In spite of all that Jacob had gone through, as he was giving his final blessings to his sons, he still recognized that God had shepherded him through his life. God had led, provided, and protected him. He also called God the one who redeemed him from evil (Genesis 48:15-16).

When Jacob blesses Joseph, he describes a battle between archers (Genesis 49:23). And in verse 24, he reminds Joseph that the strength in Joseph's arm and bow is from "the Mighty One of Israel," and then says, "from there is the Shepherd, the Stone of Israel." Isn't it interesting that the theme of God being a Shepherd and a Rock comes so early in the Bible?

In Psalm 61, David prays for God to defend and protect him and asks God to lead him to the Rock that is higher than he is.

There are times when we just need our Shepherd to take us to the safety of the Rock. We are so blessed that they are the same person, Jesus Christ. When we know Him as our Shepherd, we can know Him as our Rock.

Lead Me to the Rock – Christ Our Life

Isaiah 53:4 & 5a

There are days in everyone's life where it seems like grief and sorrows are huge mountains and we can't see the top. Isaiah reminds us here that Jesus carries our grief and sorrows. What seems completely upside down in this verse is that we look at Jesus and see that he is weighed down by grief and sorrows, and then we assume that God must have afflicted him with it. It's between them. But it's our grief and sorrows that he is carrying. That's not even half of it…

Let's break down verse 5. There is a lot to unpack here.

He was wounded for our transgressions. My translation says "pierced."

What are transgressions? Those are sins that you commit, knowingly or unknowingly.

By doing something you shouldn't or not doing what you should.

They can be private, public, or in your thoughts.

They are not mistakes. They are not errors in judgment. Let's call them what they are: they are sin.

So, when Jesus' brow was pierced with thorns, when his wrists and ankles were pierced with spikes, when his side was pierced with a spear to confirm that he really was dead…

That was to pay the penalty for those sins.

"He was crushed (bruised) for our iniquities."

What are iniquities?

Something that is iniquitous is fouled from within. It is corrupted, degenerate and reprehensible.

This isn't just what we do; it's about who we are. It is our sinful human nature that we are conceived with, that we inherited from Adam and Eve. We are helpless to do anything about it because, no matter how hard we try to do good, it's still there, lurking inside.

But Jesus, in His purity and holiness, paid for that too.

When he asked his Father to take this cup from Him because it was so heavy, he sweated blood because of the physical strain of what he knew was coming.

Every time he fell under the weight of the cross as he carried it to Golgotha, every time he slumped on the cross, and his lungs could not exhale or inhale until he lifted himself on the nail in his feet.

All of it was so he could take your iniquity and give you His righteousness.

Upon Him - Matt Redman

Isaiah 53:5b

In our last talk, we looked at Isaiah 53:4-5a. It's heavy stuff, so I thought it would be a good idea to give you a moment to think on it and then continue as we keep breaking these phrases down so we understand what Isaiah was telling us about Jesus.

"Upon Him was the chastisement that brought us peace."

What is "chastisement"?

When a person is chastised, it generally means they have been called out for what they have done. It's laying all the cards on the table and being honestly told what has happened, how it has affected the people around you, and what needs to change. And you know full well that they are right. When that has happened to me, it brings deep shame, guilt, grief, and humiliation.

The first two phrases we covered, about transgressions and iniquities, cause us to feel chastised. We know we are separated from God by our sinfulness and corrupt human nature. And we know that without Jesus taking it all on Himself, there is nothing we can do. It brings shame, guilt, and humiliation.

But this tells us that Jesus even took <u>that</u> upon Himself.

Every time he was condemned unjustly, every time he was mocked.

When he was left naked and exposed and alone on the cross, and when he asked God, his Father, why He had abandoned him to this…

He took our shame, our guilt, and our grief and, in return, He gives us peace that passes understanding. We get peace in our own human spirit. We can approach God, our Father, with confidence instead of fear and shame. We can come with confidence.

"And by his stripes (wounds) we are healed."

No hard words here, but let's mull this over for a bit.

What do we need healed?

Our physical bodies? Certainly. Past abuses that have caused pain, emotional and mental scars? Absolutely.

Our relationships with people we have hurt or who have hurt us? Definitely.

Our relationship with God? Yes.

Every time the soldiers whipped Jesus with that scourge, every time his flesh tore open, every time he was struck. Every time the crown of thorns was hit with the rod, the thorns tore open his scalp.

Every drop of blood he lost… was so that you could be healed of all the pain, all the mental anguish, all the scars and addictions. Our relationships can be brought to a place where they are resolved in our own hearts.

And yes, our relationship with God can be restored through Jesus' sacrifice on the day he died on the cross.

He really did pay it all.

Jesus Paid It All - Josh Snodgrass - Acoustic Guitar

Jesus Paid It All

Mrs. H. M. Hall, John T. Grape

I hear the Savior say, "Thy strength indeed is small,

Child of weakness, watch and pray

Find in Me thine all in all."

Refrain:

Jesus paid it all, all to him I owe

Sin had left a crimson stain

He washed it white as snow

For nothing good have I where by thy grace to claim –

I'll wash my garments white

In the blood of Calvary's Lamb

And when, before the throne, I stand in Him complete

"Jesus died my soul to save."

My lips shall still repeat.

Isaiah 53:6

Sheep have a tendency to wander off. That's how they get lost, and the shepherd has to go find the one and leave the ninety-nine behind.

Like sheep, we have a very hard time not wandering away from the Shepherd and where he wants us to be. We see the tasty morsel that is just off the path, and we end up stuck in the rocks. We see the sparkling water in the stream on the edge of the pasture and wander off to give it a taste, without the shepherd's approval, only to find that it's tainted with poison.

While you listen to "All We Like Sheep" from The Messiah, you can hear the sopranos, altos, tenors, and basses all wander off on their own paths. It's really quite delightful! And then, they all come together in the deepest minor key and remind us of the consequences of our sin, "The Lord laid on him (Jesus) the iniquity of us all." You see, our sin doesn't just have consequences for us. We're in the rocks and are sick because we're poisoned.

The consequences are also on Jesus.

He doesn't just save us and heal us; he physically took the sin on himself when he died on the cross.

All We Like Sheep Have Gone Astray - Handel's Messiah, Toronto Mendelssohn Choir, Toronto Symphony Orchestra

Isaiah 53:7

In Isaiah 53:6, we talked about us as the sheep.

Now Isaiah tells us about how Jesus will be when it's time to pay our debt. He says that Jesus was silent as a lamb before his oppressors. He didn't defend himself. He didn't crush them all with a word from his mouth, though he could have.

It certainly was not Jesus' habit to be silent. But being the perfect Son of God, he knew when and what to speak. He had no problem telling people the truth about themselves; so much so that one day the disciples asked Jesus if he knew he had offended the Pharisees (Matthew 15:10-12). If Jesus were here today, I'm sure he would say, "Yes, that was the point."

Why was Jesus silent in this situation? Of course, to fulfill Isaiah's prophecy. But also to show us an example of how to respond when we are falsely accused. If we look at 1 Peter 2:23, we see that "He entrusted himself to him who judges justly."

While Jesus was steadfastly heading to the cross, he had to trust his Father's plan.

Sometimes, we need to defend the gospel and biblical truth. Sometimes, though, we need to be quiet in the presence of false accusations and entrust ourselves to our Father, who will judge justly at the right time.

He Will Keep You - Sovereign Grace Music

It's time to read **Isaiah 53** in its entirety. Slow down and think about what Jesus did for you. Listen to **How Deep the Father's Love for Us** – Collin Hill while you read.

Other resources: Charles Christian, "The Silence of the Lamb," April 15, 2021, Christian Trends.

How Deep The Father's Love For Us

How deep the Father's love for us
How vast beyond all measure
That He would give His only Sons
To make a wretch His treasure
How great the pain of searing loss
The Father turns His face away
As wounds which mar the chosen One
Bring many sons to glory
Behold the Man upon a cross
My sin upon His shoulders
Ashamed, I hear my mocking voice
Call out among the scoffers
It was my sin that held Him there
Until it was accomplished
His dying breath has brought me life
I know that it is finished
I will not boast in anything
No gifts, no power, no wisdom
But I will boast in Jesus Christ
His death and resurrection
Why should I gain from His reward?
I cannot give an answer
But this I know with all my heart
His wounds have paid my ransom

Stuart Townsend

Exodus 12:1-28

One of the movies I remember watching as a child was "The 10 Commandments." When I read the stories of Moses in the Bible, Moses still looks like Charlton Heston! When the greenish mist crept through the towns and cities of Egypt, it was one of the scariest things I had ever seen!

God gives Moses and Aaron clear instructions for the night He plans to strike down all the firstborn in Egypt:

- Every household chooses a perfect male lamb or kid.

- If there is too much for your family, invite the neighbors.

- Take good care of the lamb for 4 days.

- On the 14th, at dusk, everyone kills their lamb.

- Take some of the blood and put it on the posts of your front door and on the support above your door.

- Roast the lamb. Eat quickly. Make sure you're ready to walk out the door.

- Burn the leftovers in the morning.

- Every year, for all your generations, do this to remember how I, and I alone, brought you out of Egypt.

God promises when He sees the blood around the door, the people inside will be spared judgment. The Hebrews had to trust what God had said, and obey, or they would suffer the loss of their firstborn, just like the Egyptians.

What a beautiful prophetic message for those who have covered their lives with the blood of Jesus, our Passover Lamb. He is the only one who can save us from the wrath of God and give us peace when everything around us is in chaos. Have you trusted and obeyed? Have you trusted Jesus' shed blood to cover and protect you? Have you invited a neighbor to experience the blessing of trusting the blood of the Lamb?

Are you ready to go when Jesus comes to get his saved ones?

O Praise the Name (Anastasis) – Shane and Shane (Live)

1 Samuel 17:34-54

David has seen Goliath challenge the Israeli army and is discussing with King Saul why he is qualified to challenge Goliath. David explains to Saul that he is a shepherd and has fought off lions and bears that attacked the flock, and this Philistine will turn out like them.

Credit goes where credit is due, and David says:

"The Lord who delivered me from the paw of the lion and the paw of the bear will deliver me from the hand of this Philistine." After a brief armor debacle, David goes and gets 5 smooth stones from the brook and puts them in his pouch... wait... why did he get 5? Didn't he think that God could do this with only one stone? Was he thinking, just in case God misses with the first one, I'll have four back-ups, and I can help with those?

I don't think so. When David talks to Goliath, he tells him exactly what is going to happen, and more importantly, who is actually doing business with Goliath. He says:

"This day, the Lord will deliver you into my hand... so all the earth will know there is a God in Israel and this assembly (Saul, the Israel army, the Philistine army) will know that the Lord saves not with sword and spear. The battle is the Lord's, and he will give you into our hand."

That sounds pretty confident in God's deliverance. So why 5 stones? It turns out that Goliath has four relations that are also giants. (2 Samuel 21:15-22).

I would think they were there on the battlefield backing up their very big relative. David was prepared not only to take out Goliath but also the other 4 giants as well!

How often do I think I need to have everything ready to help God when he fails the first time? Yes, I need to be prepared for the battles that I need to fight with sin, temptation, and opposition, but do I truly believe that God can take out the giants with only one stone?

Am I giving Him the glory when the enemies are defeated?

How do we get ready for the battle? We pray, we give God the glory, we put on all the armor God has given us (Ephesians 6:10-20).

The Battle Belongs – Phil Wickham

John 1:29-34

Behold the Lamb of God.

John the Baptist and Jesus had not spent any time together as they were growing up, in spite of being second cousins. John had recognized the presence of Jesus when their mothers were together and both pregnant, but that was apparently the last time they were together.

By the time this passage occurs, John has a very clear understanding of his role. He knows that he is the one who cries out in the wilderness: "Make straight the way of the Lord."

He knows that Jesus is far above him. He knows Jesus is eternal. He knows that he has a role in revealing Jesus to Israel. He has seen the Holy Spirit come and remain on Jesus at baptism. And he knows exactly what Jesus is there to do:

"Behold, the Lamb who takes away the sin of the world."

It isn't too much longer, and John the Baptist has been jailed. He sends a couple of disciples to ask Jesus if he is really the Messiah. Should we be looking for someone else? (Matthew 11:1-6). Jesus confirms that he is exactly who John proclaimed him to be.

What happened to John? He proclaimed Jesus to be the Lamb of God with full conviction, and now he's not sure if he was right. John came under serious persecution for his belief in Jesus and ended up in prison. When things in our lives get very hard, it can lead to questioning if Jesus really is who He says He is. We feel alone and abandoned and find it hard to trust our own thoughts. That's when we must look at Jesus again and know that he does exactly what the prophets said he would do.

The blind see.

The lame walk.

The lepers are cleansed.

The poor are encouraged.

I have had my sins taken away.

I have peace.

I have been given life.

And when life is hard, I can say again, with confidence, "Look, it's Jesus, the Lamb of God! He took away my sin, and He can take away yours, too."

This We Know – Vertical Worship

John 10:1-30

"I am the good shepherd, I know my own and my own know me."

There are so many times in the Gospels where Jesus explained something to his disciples using a figure of speech or a parable, and the disciples did not understand. I can relate. So, Jesus explains it further, sometimes in a straightforward manner, but he often will take the same parable and expand it, as he does here, or give examples with other stories.

In this passage, Jesus is telling the people about his relationship with those who follow him, and he uses the example of a shepherd and his sheep. In two of Jesus' "I AM" statements, he calls himself "The door for the sheep" and "The Good Shepherd."

Let's look at the thieves, strangers and hired hands first:

The person who tries to sneak in the back way is a thief. His goal is to steal, kill and destroy the sheep

Sheep will not follow a stranger; they don't know him or recognize his voice, and will run away

Hired hands who don't own the sheep will run at the first sign of trouble and abandon the sheep to the wolves.

The relationship between the Good Shepherd and His Sheep:

- The Good Shepherd comes through the door. There is no need to sneak in the back.

- The Good Shepherd calls his sheep by their names. He knows each one and sees them all individually.

- The sheep hear and know the shepherd's voice. They follow him alone because that is the voice they trust.

- The sheep come into the fold only through the one door that the shepherd opens for them. The Shepherd leads them in and out and finds pastures for them.

- The Good Shepherd lays down his life for his sheep. He will die to save them from the wolves.

- He knows his sheep, and his sheep know him.

He longs to gather all of his sheep together so the whole flock can be with their one Shepherd.

As sheep, we must listen to and recognize our Shepherd's voice. How do we do that? We spend time with Him, read his word, and trust where he leads us.

If you are not sure you are listening to the Shepherd, talk to other sheep that you know hear him.

Jesus laid down his life for us, and he had the authority to take his life back. Because of that authority, he has given us eternal life; we will never perish, and no one can take us out of his hand. His Father gave him to him, and we cannot be taken away.

The Good Shepherd - Tommy Walker Ministries (2017)

John 21:15-17

After Jesus' resurrection, he appeared to his disciples several times. The third time, the men are out fishing, and Jesus calls to them from the beach. They had caught nothing, and Jesus told them to put the net over the other side of the boat. At that point, they know who it is on the beach. They've seen this scenario before! When Jesus first called his disciples, they had exactly the same conversation (Matthew 4:18-22).

Once the men are on shore, Jesus invites them to contribute to the breakfast he has already prepared. When they are settled, he has a conversation with Peter. Now Peter is probably still broken-hearted about denying Jesus during the trial. When the rooster crowed, the guilt and shame for the next several weeks would have haunted him. This one-on-one conversation could not have been easy.

Jesus asks Peter, "Do you love me?"

Jesus is asking about a self-sacrificing, all-consuming love.

Peter responds with, "You know that I love you." But the response is of brotherly love, not as deep, not as transcendent, as what Jesus asked.

This exchange happened three times, and each time, Jesus responded with:

- "Feed My lambs"
- "Tend My sheep"
- "Feed My sheep"

Be a shepherd to my followers. Nourish the young. Keep the mature healthy. Guard them. Protect them. Keep them moving in the right direction. Make sure every single one gets home to the safety of the fold when it's time.

This is a daunting call. Did Peter even understand at the time what Jesus was asking? We know that within weeks, he suddenly had a flock of 3000 or so sheep and lambs. Without the strength of the Holy Spirit to guide and help, he would have been overwhelmed.

My calling from Jesus seems small in comparison:

- I am to be a Christ-like woman, wife, mom, and friend.

- I am to help lead his people in worship.

- I am to run a business in an honest, upright way and care for my young staff.

To do these things, I must rely on the Holy Spirit to guide and help, or I would be utterly overwhelmed. Some days I am. Then I remember: Jesus has not left me alone to figure this out for myself. I have Him, the Spirit, the Word, and the Father. They feed and tend me.

You Are My Strength - Hillsong Worship

Mark 6:30-34

Do you ever do something new and it's exciting and exhausting, and even though it's been so good, you are so tired? Maybe a family vacation, or a big service project. Each Christmas I have head the preparation of grocery hampers for people connected to our congregation. It's about three weeks of planning and answering questions. Then there are three days of really hard work! And then one day, when I really just want a nap. It's great! It's satisfying! It's exhausting!

Jesus had sent his disciples out on their first mission trip. They came home and were excited about all they had done and seen, but these men were tired. Jesus suggests they get away by themselves so the disciples have a chance to rest. But the crowds figured out where they were going and went ahead to meet them. When Jesus and his men get off the boat, there they are... no rest for anyone today. Verse 34 says, "When He went ashore, he saw a great crowd, and he had compassion on them, because they were like sheep without a shepherd."

Jesus' compassion for people is so very evident throughout his ministry. How often do you see him healing, teaching, and caring, while others around him see the people he is caring for as an interruption, an intrusion, unworthy of his attention, or unclean and untouchable? But Jesus' compassion moved him to see them, love them, heal them, and draw near to them.

How often do I see someone as an intrusion or unworthy of my attention? Do I let my tiredness, my emotions or my busy-ness get in the way of caring for someone that God placed in my path? More often than I would care to admit.

Prayer:

Jesus, please forgive me for not having the same compassion for people that you do. Help me to see them, care for them, and love them the way that you would.

Jesus, Full of Compassion - Caroline Cobb (2021)

Revelation 5

As John was receiving the Revelation of Jesus, at one point, God the Father had a seven-sealed scroll in his hand, and John began to weep, as no one could be found who was worthy to open the scroll. The angel comes to him and comforts him with these words:

"Weep no more; behold, the Lion of the tribe of Judah, the Root of David, has conquered, so he can open the scroll and its seven seals."

Now, I don't know what picture that draws to your mind. Perhaps a mighty warrior, or a Narnia-like lion, or a king clothed in glorious garments. It doesn't bring to mind a slaughtered lamb. Yet that is how Jesus comes to accept the scroll from the hand of God, his Father. Jesus' death on the cross, being the sacrifice for the sin of the world, providing redemption for his people and then overcoming death was the defining act of history, so he comes to open the seals of judgement as the Lamb of God

And then all of heaven bursts into praise!

"Worthy is the Lamb to receive power, wealth, wisdom and might and honor and glory and blessing… forever and ever!"

What a moment it will be. My own acts of worship are a small pittance of what it will be like when we are there to praise and thank him for all he has done. Take a moment and worship the Lamb, Jesus, who is worthy of all you can give him.

All Glory - Vertical Worship

Psalm 23

I was asked to sing at a wedding, and there was a mixed quartet singing a few songs as part of the prelude. One of the ladies read the following, and it was such a beautiful description of our relationship with our Lord, our Shepherd, that I needed to share it.

The Lord is my Shepherd	That's Relationship
I shall not want	That's Supply
He makes me lie down in green pastures	That's Rest
He leads me beside still waters	That's Refreshment
He restores my soul	That's Healing
He leads me in paths of righteousness	That's Guidance
For His names' sake	That's Purpose
Even though I walk through the valley of the shadow of death	That's Testing
I will fear no evil	That's Protection
For you are with me	That's Faithfulness
Your rod and your staff, they comfort me	That's Discipline
You prepare a table for me in the presence of my enemies	That's Hope
You anoint my head with oil	That's Consecration

My cup overflows	That's Abundance
Surely goodness and mercy shall follow me all the days of my life	That's Blessing
And I shall dwell in the house of the Lord	That's Security
Forever	That's Eternity

Psalm 23 – Phil Wickham, Tiffany Hudson

Other resources: Reading by Annley Wilson

Psalm 49

When the rich young ruler left Jesus behind because he was not willing to leave his wealth behind, Jesus said, "It is easier for a camel to go through the eye of a needle than for a rich person to enter the kingdom of God." Matthew 19:24. I hope that young man went home and read Psalm 49.

The psalmist starts by calling everyone, rich or poor, to listen as he sorts out the riddle placed before us.

Why should I fear when the people who trust wealth and are willing to cheat to get more, are the ones who are sinning? Vs 5-6

Verses 8-13 say it doesn't matter if you are wise, foolish, wealthy, pompous or arrogant; we all die and end up in the grave. As in the proverbial, 'You can't take it with you', verse 10 makes it clear that all you accumulate gets left behind for others who 'approve of their boasts'. 'He was quite a businessman! What a generous guy to leave all of this to us!' They never give a thought to where he might be now.

They are like sheep all being herded to the same place, Sheol. Verse 14

We shouldn't worry when a person becomes rich. The glory he has gained here stays here when he dies. If he has no understanding, his life just leads to death and darkness.

So, what does he need to understand?

He needs to understand that no person can pay God enough to buy eternal life for himself or anyone else. It is just too costly. Verses 7-9. He needs to understand that the upright will ultimately rule in God's kingdom, and that only God himself can ransom his soul from hell and death. Verses 14-15.

What a perfect segue to tell people about the saving grace of Jesus's death on the cross. We are lost hopelessly in our sin, hoping we can do something to save ourselves. But God incarnate, Jesus Christ, gave himself to die in our place. To ransom us from the grave by dying on the cross. Jesus is the only path to eternal life.

Which shepherd are you being led by? You can let death be your shepherd, who will lead you to hell. Or you can place your life in the hands of the Good Shepherd, who laid down his own life to ransom his sheep.

Blessed – Vertical Worship

James 3

Every few years, a memory pops up on my Facebook page that says;

A tidbit of wisdom from a kind cashier this morning. "You can't say anything you'll regret with a mouthful of chocolate."

I don't remember the circumstances or who I was mad at on January 29, 2016, but the copious amounts of chocolate I purchased and my demeanor must have said it all.

Oh, the tongue. It's nearly impossible to find anywhere in the Bible that has anything good to say about it. Jesus said it's not what goes into a man's mouth that defiles him, but what comes out of it, Matthew 15:11. In only four verses, James calls our tongues;

A fire, set on fire by hell

A world of unrighteousness

It stains the whole body

Untameable

A restless evil

Full of deadly poison

Ouch!

He uses the examples of a bit in a horse's mouth and a ship's rudder to show us that a small thing like our tongue can control the direction we go. Now, we understand that he isn't talking about our physical tongue. He's talking about how we use it to speak words that are cruel, unkind, slanderous, full of gossip, rumours and anger.

So, how do we get this unruly tongue under control? As with most of our spiritual walk, it starts with what is in our hearts. Fill your heart with 'wisdom that comes from above. It is pure, gentle. peaceable, open to reason, full of mercy and good fruit, impartial and sincere.' If these things are in your heart and mind, it's much less likely something ugly will come out of your mouth.

And it's much better for you than stuffing your mouth with chocolate!

Rumormill – Featuring Jon Mohr, Live

Psalm 19

Back in about 1997, I was in a situation where I needed to have a meeting in our church with about 20 angry parents. I was the Children's Ministry Director, and there was a particular area that we were having problems with. I had sent out notices, called meetings, and put out a survey of questions to discuss at our annual meeting. No response, nothing changed. So, I created a series of policies that needed to be followed, and all of a sudden, there was a RESPONSE! I had done my due diligence, had the support of the pastor, but I knew I was walking into a room where it was me versus them. I was hurt, angry, and didn't want to say something that would make the situation worse or that I would regret later.

I happened to read Psalm 19 that day, and it spoke to where I was and gave me a solution to my fear of saying the wrong thing. The psalm ends with:

"May the words of my mouth and the meditation of my heart be pleasing in your sight, O Lord, my rock and my redeemer."

I memorized it, repeated it to myself what seemed like a hundred times during the meeting, and wrote it at the top of the page in my notebook. It was my plea to God, asking him not let me open my mouth and say something stupid! I survived the meeting. I won't say I became friends with anyone there, but we were able to work together toward a solution.

The first two sections of the Psalm are simple praise. Verses 1-6 are about how the heavens declare God's glory.

Verses 1-11 are all about God's word. It's perfect, sure, right, pure, true, clean, and more precious than gold. For those who love it, it is sweeter than honey. Verse 11 also reminds us that there are plenty of warnings! And there are rewards for keeping God's laws

Verse 12 asks, "Who can discern his (own) errors?" Sometimes we think we're right, but we have justified our thoughts so much that we may be wrong and not even recognize it anymore.

David then asks God to declare him "innocent of hidden faults." I don't think David is referring to sins we have deliberately hidden. He is asking for forgiveness for sins he didn't even realize he committed.

Then in verse 13, he asks God to hold him back from "presumptuous sins." What are those? These are sins that we commit.

To be presumptuous, according to the Oxford Dictionary, is to "fail to observe the limits of what is permitted or appropriate." Similar words are brazen, overconfident, and arrogant. So, following the line of thought from verse 12:

I may think I am right, but if I am not, please, Lord, keep me from doing something in overconfidence that causes me to sin. And don't allow me to be controlled by pride, arrogance, or presumptuousness. Then I will be blameless and avoid sin.

So, Lord, may the words I speak, the thoughts I think, and the motives of my heart be pleasing in your sight. (v. 14) If those 3 things are in line with what pleases God, we don't have to worry about sin overtaking us. I am so grateful that Jesus is my Rock and my Redeemer. When I ask for forgiveness, He is there, ready to forgive. When I ask for help to avoid sin, He steps in and helps.

Here's My Heart – Official Live Performance, Casting Crowns

Psalm 20

In many churches, at the end of the service, the Pastor will finish with a benediction. It is a passage of scripture that asks God's blessing over His people.

Psalm 20 is beautiful poetry and has the form of a benediction. Let's look at what David is blessing his people with.

Verses 1-3: "May the Lord answer you."

This makes an assumption that you have called out to Him, in this case, for support, protection, and help when there is trouble. David also reminds us of what we need to do our part by obeying what He has asked us to do. Offerings and sacrifices were part of God's law, and people could not expect His blessing if they refused to obey.

Verses 4-6: I've always had a bit of trouble understanding verses like verse 4. "May He grant you the desires of your heart and fulfill all your plans." My heart does not always desire the very good things. In fact, sometimes it's selfish and sinful, and I would never want God to grant me those things. However, when my heart is in line with God's heart, the things it desires will be good things that bless others.

Verses 6-9: I love passages that start with "I know". There is such confidence in those statements.

What do we know here? The Lord saves those He anoints. He hears and answers our prayers. He will save us. We can trust Him. We can stand with His strength. Verse 7: "Some trust in chariots and some in horses, but we trust in the name of the Lord our God."
He Will Hold Me Fast – Selah

Colossians 1:21-29

You know how moms have that uncanny ability to just know where things are? When my kids were little, they wouldn't be able to find things, even though I would tell them exactly where they were.

The best one, though, was when my daughter was frantically looking for something.

Her: "Mom, I can't find m…"

Me: I held up a finger to stop her mid-sentence, looked her in the eye and said, "Between the second and third cushions on the couch."

Her: "But it's my…"

Me: Stopped her again. "Second and third cushions." Pointed at the couch.

Her: Goes to the couch, reaches between the second and third cushions and pulls out her car keys. Looks at her brother and says, "How does she do that??!! It freaks me out!"

The day before, I had sat down, felt something unusual, reached down between the cushions and felt the keys. I didn't know if they were the sons' or the daughters', but I knew that someone was going to be looking for those keys soon. I left the keys there.

When she reads this, it will be the first time she will know the whole story. As a parent, sometimes withholding some information is a good thing. It can help to teach lessons, like keep your keys where you can find them. It gives you a bit of an edge when they think you can do the impossible!

Sometimes it's because what you know is too much for them to handle at their stage of life.

And occasionally, you want to make sure all of the pieces are in place before you reveal the mystery.

Paul and many of the other apostles and disciples had the joy of revealing the 'mystery hidden for ages and generations.' Verse 26. That through the work of Jesus on the cross, his life could be ours. And that it wasn't only for the Jews, but also for the Gentiles!

There are hints of the mystery throughout the Old Testament, but God the Father waited until all of the pieces were in place before revealing it completely.

Call On the Name – Vertical Worship

1 Corinthians 3:4-9

I decided to plant a few veggies in my patio planters at the ice cream store this year. I rigged up a trellis for some cucumbers with great hopes of lots of tzatziki sauce later this summer. I waited patiently for the weather to get warm enough to put plants out, went to my favorite greenhouse, and they had not one single cucumber plant left. I went to the second one, where I found the last three little bedraggled cucumber plants. They were leggy, wilted and a bit on the yellowish side, but it was all they had, so I bought them. I planted them in what was supposed to be "good Saskatchewan topsoil", but it seemed to be mostly sand and rocks; too dense to really grow anything well.

Things did not go well. Two of them could not overcome how poor they were when they went in the ground. The last little plant still had one green leaf, so I placed my tzatziki hopes in him. A few days later, I discovered a new shipment of cucumber plants and picked up some to replace their fallen comrades. They seem to be doing well!

But my one-leafed cucumber plant was just sitting there, pretty much exactly like it was on the first day. As of today, he has been in that spot for three weeks, and I noticed that his one leaf was turning yellow around the edges…but…on closer inspection… he had grown a new, tiny leaf!

I planted and watered, but God has given the growth!

Maybe you have a friend or family member who isn't a Christian, or they are, but they aren't living for Jesus. You've planted seeds or baby plants. You've prayed. You've shared the gospel. It looks like nothing is happening. Maybe it even looks like they are going backwards. But one day, God, who gives the growth, may surprise you with a new, little leaf.

So don't give up; keep planting and watering and praying. Keep building into them with all the good things God can offer. You might not ever get to see the results, but you need to trust God for the growth.

Dream Small – The Stoltzfus Family

Jeremiah 36

Many of us would agree that we are living in a time when the Word of God is dismissed and disdained.

It's old wives' stories that have no actual truth.

It doesn't line up with my philosophy of life, so I don't find it relevant.

None of that absurd miracle stuff could actually happen; it's not scientifically possible.

It was all written so long ago that it can't possibly have any cultural significance now.

If there is a God, he certainly isn't interested in making *my* world a better place for *me*, so why should I care?

It's just a bunch of words written by regular people that I can't even understand most of the time, so it's worthless.

Jeremiah's scribe, Baruch, wrote down what God told Jeremiah and then read it in the synagogue, just as God had said. Then he was taken to the officials and he read it again. The officials at least reacted with fear (vs 16). They recognized that Jeremiah was God's prophet and decided the king needed to hear this.

Jehudi reads the scroll to King Jehoiakim, and as he reads it, the king mocks the word of God. "Why would he say we'll be destroyed? That's ridiculous. None of this will happen. (Vs 29)" Then the king systematically cut off portions of the scroll as it was being read and burned it!

The pride and audacity it would take to do that! Not only did God's prophetic pronouncement happen, but the evil king who burned the word of God received extra punishment.

The world we live in is dark right now, and it seems like everyone is okay with every thought and philosophy out there…except anything that is actually biblical. And many who say they believe the Bible really only want the nice, easy, loving parts.

Anything that convicts the heart of sin is judgmental.

Any part calling a thought or action a sin is condemning.

Anything warning of punishment for sin, they dismiss, like Jehoiakim, "That won't happen."

And parts that imply the God of the universe has a personal interest and influence on their day-to-day life; those parts are ridiculous! Why would he? And if he does, they are not interested.

Pride, selfishness and self-sufficiency have robbed them of a full, abundant life in Christ.

If Jehoiakim had repented and fallen in humility before God, would it have changed what happened? I don't know. At least, it would have shown belief in God's word.

Don't dismiss the hard parts of your Bible. They are there to teach and build and grow you and to keep you set apart for God.

Is He Worthy? – Chris Tomlin (2018)

Isaiah 45:14-25

What do you trust for your salvation? I hope the answer is obvious. There are lots of things you could misplace your trust in that will fail every time.

Will wealth and 'stuff' save you? No. vs 14

Will authority over people save you? No. vs 14

An idol is anything you turn to other than God when things get hard, or something that consumes your time, money and energy. Your television, your social media, your job, your house, etc., will these man-made idols save you? No. vs 16 and 20

Will science save you? No. vs 18

Will knowledge, intelligence and logic save you? No. vs 20&21

Who can tell you long ago what will happen in the future? Only God. vs 21

Who can promise something, with no other witnesses or supporting evidence needed, and we know without a doubt it is righteous and true? Only God. Vs 23

God makes it very clear in this passage that there is salvation only in Him!

Jesus told us the only way to the Father is through him. "I am the Way, the truth and the Life. No one comes to the Father except through Me." John 14:6

Take a look at the last part of verse 23. Does it sound familiar? Read Philippians 2:9-11. Here, it explains that Jesus' death on the cross opens the way to the Father. And then… "At the name of

Jesus every knee shall bow, in heaven and on earth and under the earth, and every tongue confess that Jesus Christ is Lord, to the glory of God the Father."

God's Word is amazing!!

A King Like This – Chris Tomlin

1 John 2:7-14

If you just read verses 7 and 8 and don't stop to think about them, this passage is really confusing. Is this a new commandment or not, Pastor John? Please be more clear.

In short, the word that they had, what we call the Old Testament, is full of value for teaching us, instructing us and showing us God's plan. But there is a newness to the commandments, because now we have the light of Jesus living within us as the Holy Spirit, and he helps us understand the Old Testament more completely.

From the context of the verses about loving versus hating our brother, I think we can safely surmise that John is referring to Leviticus 19:18, "You shall not take vengeance or bear a grudge against the sons of your own people, but you shall love your neighbour as yourself: I am the Lord."

If we are living in the darkness, we are prone to stumbling, we are blind, we don't know where we are going, and we hate our brothers. But now that Jesus is in us, the darkness is dissipating, and we can know where we are going, we can see clearly, and we love our brothers and sisters in the Lord with love that Jesus gives us.

Verses 12-14 are considered by commentators to be about our spiritual growth.

As spiritual children, the basics of our faith are at the forefront. Our sins are forgiven, and we are getting to know the Father.

As spiritual youth, we are growing, abiding in the word and learning to overcome the evil one and the temptations he brings.

As adult believers, we have matured and have come to know Jesus and the Father.

As Jesus' light lives in us, we need to continue to grow in love for our brothers and sisters in Christ and in spiritual maturity.

Keep Shining, my Friends!!

Lord, Shine Your Light – Elevating Gospel Worship 2024

Psalm 25

On his children's programme, Mr. Rogers used to sing a song, "Let's think of something to do while we're waiting." What do you do while you're waiting for something? I have a couple of family members who like to phone me while they wait for things. Some people listen to music, read a book or just sit there and get annoyed. In Psalm 25, David gives us some suggestions on what to do while we are waiting.

First, let's figure out what David was waiting for. In verses 3, 5 and 21, he says, "I will wait for you." 'You' refers to the Lord. David, you and I both know that God is with us, so he must have been waiting for God to do something.

What is David waiting for God to do?

For God to prevent him from being put to shame or exulted over by his enemies. V 2&3

To be taught and led in God's ways. V 4&5

For God to remember that He is merciful and good. And to please forget the sins of my youth. V 6&7

For the Lord to save him from the net he is tangled in. V 150

For the Lord to turn toward him and bring him out of distress. V 16&17

Forgiveness of his sin. V 18

For God to guard and deliver him. V 19&20

Preservation V 21

That's a lot of things to wait for God to do. Some are very personal, like forgiving my sins. Some are more public, like not letting me be put to shame. I think the point is that God doesn't always answer our prayers instantly. He doesn't fix hard situations immediately. He doesn't always save us from trouble right away. He doesn't show us which way to go, or his whole plan, all at once. Often, He makes us wait a while so we grow and learn to trust Him and His ways.

Now, what did David tell us to do while we are waiting?

We lift up our souls to God. We give ourselves and open our hearts to what He has for us. V 1

We trust Him. We acknowledge that He is God, and we are not, and choose to trust Him. V 2

We learn God's ways. How do we do that? Get into His word. If we understand how God works, then waiting for Him to act doesn't seem like such a chore. We learn that his timing is always perfect. V 4&5

We confess our sin. Keep short accounts with God, so when He is ready to work in a situation, you are ready to see it happen. V7

Stay humble. V 9

Obey His word. V 10

Fear the Lord. Remember that God is holy, and he will give you peace as you wait. If we understand what it means to fear the Lord, He offers us His friendship!! Read verse 14 again! V 10-14

Keep your eyes on Jesus. V 15

Bring your hurt, pain and problems to God. Praying for healing/deliverance/direction/resolution isn't a once-and-done thing. Continue to bring it to Him in prayer, not because he forgets about it, but because he wants you to stay in a relationship with Him. V 16 & 18

Take refuge in Him. Sometimes all we can do is ask Him to cover and protect us. V 20

Continue in integrity and righteousness. V 21

Do you have things you are waiting for God to take care of? Instead of asking why it's taking so long, now you have a list of things to do while you're waiting!

While I'm Waiting – John Waller

Psalm 37

My daughter surprised me with a trip to New York in January a few years ago. She had lived in Melbourne, Australia, for a couple of years and was well acquainted with the traffic challenges of a metropolitan center. I had lived in a city of 17,000 for 30 years.

After we got out of the airport, we made our way to the airport bus terminal to get on a bus to take us into the city. We were almost there and had to cross the street to get on the bus. The walk light was yellow, and she went quickly and confidently across the street. I hesitated. Then I panicked. Then I ran across the street in front of a moving bus. Then my daughter (and the bus driver!) panicked. She firmly admonished me and finished with, "How am I supposed to keep you alive in the city for a week if you do things like that?!"

I learned very quickly to stick close, go when she went, stop when she stopped and by week's end, I was crossing the street almost like a seasoned New Yorker!

This psalm is a contrast between what happens to the righteous and what happens to the wicked. Look at what happens when the righteous follow the Lord in His ways.

Commit your way to the Lord, and He will act! V 5

Sometimes we need to be still and wait patiently. Just stay put until He moves. V 7

When you are joyful in the way God is leading, he gives confidence in your steps and lifts you up when you fall. V 23 & 24

Turn away from evil. A good indicator that you need a direction change is when you recognize something is evil. Time to turn the corner! V 27

If you keep God's word in your heart, your steps will be sure. V 31

Keep God's way, and wait for Him to work. There is a reward when you do. V 34

If you feel like you are running in front of a spiritual bus in a panic, stop and wait for God to direct your steps.

Step by Step – Rich Mullins

Romans 8:26-30

When I was 15, I met my biological father for the first time. It was awkward. Bob was drinking heavily at the time and was not a person I wanted to get to know. Over the years, there were a few phone calls, but our relationship was left at that.

When I was 32, one of his sons, my half-brother, died unexpectedly, and for some reason, Bob wanted me to come to the funeral. I went and got to know some of my aunts and uncles and reconnected with Bob. He was still drinking, but not as heavily, and he genuinely appreciated the time we spent together.

As we got to know each other, it was fascinating to me to see how much genetics played a role in how I function, and in ways I never expected. We had similar facial expressions. We both ended a sarcastic one-liner with the same vocal inflection. Neither of us could talk without using our hands.

As it turned out, in some ways, I was like my father, even though I hadn't grown up with him around.

The Holy Spirit that dwells within us has several jobs. He is our Comforter. Our Guide, Our Strength, and our Prayer Warrior. He also helps us become more Christ-like. He bears witness with our spirits that we are children of God, fellow heirs with Christ.' Romans 8:12-17

We are now part of the family and as such, should have the characteristics of our Father and his son, Jesus. Verse 29 says Jesus is the firstborn of many brothers (and sisters), and the Father is conforming us to the image of his Son. Now that doesn't mean that we will physically look like Jesus. It does mean that his character shows up as we live out our faith. Our gestures, our expressions, how we speak and act should look a little more like Jesus every day.

I didn't have very long to get to know Bob. His son had died in August, Bob was diagnosed with lung cancer the following February, and he passed away in August. I had the opportunity to share the gospel with him, and I think he put his faith in Jesus. I will be watching for him on my first day in heaven!

Meanwhile, I am going to keep letting the Father make me look more like Jesus.

Oh, To Be Like Thee – Melissa Schworer

Psalm 40

When I was 13, I was quite sick with something that would cause me to faint several times a day. After mounds of blood tests, multiple scans of every kind, tests of everything, I was finally diagnosed with something quite rare. The doctors didn't know what to do to fix it, and I went through everything they could think of, including 2 spinal taps, one of which left me in bed and barely able to move for 3 days.

I spent a lot of time with my music during those months, and one song that meant so much was Evie's "Part the Water." I never knew what a day would bring, and more than once I felt like I was going under.

When I think I'm going under, part the waters, Lord.

When I feel the waves around me, calm the sea.

When I cry for help, O hear me, Lord, and hold out your hand.

Touch my life, still the raging storm in me.

We all have seasons of our lives that are overwhelming. Maybe it's an illness, the death of a loved one, a broken relationship you can do nothing to fix, or a financial burden that feels like a rock slide. You know what those things are for you. That's when you hold up your hand and cry to Jesus to take it and pull you up.

When you are poor and needy, Jesus knows, and He will help and deliver.

Part the Waters – Evie

Psalm 42

Psalm 42 was likely written while David was on the run from King Saul, so there is a swing from longing to hope, questioning to assurance, and depression to trust.

David's heart longs for God; he desperately wants to come and worship at the temple:

When shall I come and appear before God? **v2**
I would lead the procession to the house of God **v4**
I shall again praise Him. **v5 & 11**

***

David's adversaries ask, "Where is your God?" David remembers:

Worship at the temple **v4**
God can be seen and heard anywhere **v6**

***

David's soul is "cast down." He states:

"I shall hope in God; He is my salvation." **v5**
Though he cries day and night, he knows the Lord steadfastly loves him in the day, and his songs are prayers to God in the night. **v3 & 8**

***

Even when he is overwhelmed by the flood of what is happening in his life, he knows that God is his rock.

Are you having a hard day? Are you struggling with depression? Are you overwhelmed by your circumstances?

Let God fill the longing in your heart like water quenches thirst.

Worship Him, even when you feel like you can't. He will listen to your songs and your prayers.

Remember who God is. He is your hope, your salvation, your rock. He is your God.

We Come – Keith Kitchen

Psalm 46

Many of the psalms have contrasting word pictures to help us understand more about who God is. Psalm 46 is no exception.

Verses 1 & 2 tell us, "God is our refuge and our strength, a very present help in trouble. Therefore, we will not fear…"

The first 'trouble' we run into sounds like a major earthquake. Being in the mountains in an earthquake when the earth is giving way and trembling would be terrifying. So would being near the ocean with a tsunami coming. But God is our refuge and our strength, therefore we will not fear. I don't know. I think I would be more than fearful.

The next trouble is when 'the nations rage and kingdoms totter." When nations start raging and there is political unrest, it starts to get frightening. Imagine being in Israel after the October 7, 2023, attacks. Fear of other nations sending missiles at you constantly. Fear that people you love are dead, mourning and grief on a national level. But God is our refuge and strength; we will not fear. I'm not so sure.

Remember, this psalm was written about 3000 years ago, yet it sounds like today. Natural disasters and political chaos are worse than most of us have ever seen before. Verses 8 & 9 tell us that even though the world we are in is sometimes terrifying and chaotic, God is still in control. Come and see what God is doing! I'm feeling a little better now.

Verses 4, 5, 7 and 11 remind us that God is on his throne. He is not surprised at what is happening, and He will help us. He is our fortress; the safest place we can be. Okay, take a deep breath and remember who your refuge and strength is.

Verse 10 is God speaking to us. He tells us that He will be exalted among the nations and in the earth. And He tells us to stop and remember who He is. He is sovereign. He is on His throne.

When everything feels scary and chaotic around us, the best thing we can do is be still and know that He is God.

Be Still and Know – Instrumental Worship Ensemble

Lyrics are on the following page

Be Still

Be still and know that He is God
Be still and know that He is holy
Be still, oh, restless soul of mine
Bow before the Prince of Peace
Let the noise and clamor cease

Be still and know that He is God
Be still and know that He is faithful
Consider all that He has done
Stand in awe and be amazed
And know that He will never change
Be still

Be still and know that He is God
Be still and know that He is God
Be still and know that He is God
Be still, be speechless

Be still and know that He is God
Be still and know He is our Father
Come rest your head upon His chest
Listen to the rhythm of
His unfailing heart of love
Beating for his little ones
Calling each of us to come
Be still, be still

By Steven Curtis Chapman
Copyright BMG Platinum Songs o/b/o Peach Hill Songs, BMG Platinum Songs
o/b/o BMG Rights Management (Uk) Ltd, and Capitol Cmg Genesis

Psalm 47

Reasons to Worship God Today

God is worthy of my reverent respect

God is the great King over all the earth

He is in control of what comes against me

He has an inheritance ready for me

He is proud of me!

He loves me

He is triumphant

He accepts my praise, my worship and my songs

He reigns over the nations

He is still on his throne, and He is sovereign

He gathers his people together

He will shield me

He is highly exalted

All good reasons! Add a few of your own and worship him today!!

Clap Your Hands (Psalm 47) – Live, Shane and Shane, Kingdom Kids

The Armor of God

Ephesians 6:10-20

Paul had seen his fair share of Roman guards. He was hauled in front of magistrates, kings and eventually Caesar, so men in armor were not uncommon for him. If you notice in verse 20, he was chained and in prison as he wrote this letter to the Ephesian church. Lots of guards there!

If you want somebody to remember something you are telling them, you put it at the end of your speech. Paul ends his letter to this church, telling them to be strong and how to do it.

"Be strong in the Lord and in the strength of His might."

Spiritual strength has nothing to do with how much you can bench press or how big a person you can take out in arm wrestling. It has everything to do with our relationship with Jesus. It's his strength we rely on by putting on the armor he has provided. If we were wrestling flesh and blood, maybe we could bulk up enough to take them out, but that's not the case here.

Our opponents are the 'rulers, authorities and cosmic powers of this present darkness and spiritual forces of evil.' No matter how filled with the Spirit or spiritually mature I am, I can't take those on by myself. It's only through Jesus that we can overcome those foes.

Verse 13 starts with 'therefore.' Because our battle is a spiritual one, we need God's armor to fight it. And once we have all of it on, then stand! Don't retreat, don't let your knees shake, don't get ahead of your Commander-in-Chief, don't panic. Stand firm.

What is the armor? We'll dig deeper into each one, but here is the overview:

- The belt of truth

- The breastplate of righteousness

- Your shoes are the gospel of peace

- The shield of faith

- The helmet of salvation

- The sword of the Spirit

Okay! I'm dressed. I'm standing. Now what?

Pray. Pray at all times. Pray in the Spirit. Pray with perseverance. Pray with supplication (1) for the body of Christ. Pray that people will boldly proclaim the gospel.

Stay strong, stay standing, stay in your armor, pray. And remember, above all else, Jesus' strength and power covers you. You are ultimately safe in him, no matter the enemy.

You've Already Won -Shane and Shane, Live

(1) Supplication is to earnestly and humbly ask or beg for something.

John 8:31-32/John 14:1-6

Belts are great. They hold up your pants, or they can add the finishing touch to your outfit. But when we are talking about armor, a belt is a wide piece of heavy leather, sometimes covered with metal scales to protect your lower abdomen and lower back. There are a lot of important organs there you need to stay alive!

The first thing Paul tells us to put on is the belt of truth. This is not just being a truthful person; this is knowing the truth and living it!

What is the truth? Let's see if I can take a philosophical question and simplify the answer. The truth is not something subjective. It has become a catch phrase in the last 20 years or so to say, 'My truth is…' If your truth is not truth for everyone, then it is simply not the truth. You can decide that the sky is orange, but just because you call it orange, that doesn't change the fact that the sky is blue, according to common knowledge and standard language.

For us as Christians, we have an advantage in what truth is. We have the scripture and know that truth is not something we come up with ourselves. The truth is, first of all, in Jesus words. John 8:31-32 says, "If you abide in my word, you will know the truth, and the truth will set you free." As the perfect, holy Son of God, we know that Jesus cannot lie, so we can stand on his word as the truth. This gives us freedom! I don't have to struggle with the chains of self-doubt or be caught in inconsistency, because I can go to the Word with my questions and know that if Jesus said it, it is the truth.

In John 14:1-6, Jesus is in the Upper Room with his disciples, giving them the last instructions. Within 24 hours, he will be dead, his work on earth completed. He tells them that once he is alive, he will be going back to the Father's house to prepare a place for them, and that he will come and get them to be with him. I always appreciate Thomas when he speaks up in the Bible. He usually says what we are all thinking, but are afraid to say. "We don't know where you are going. How can we know the way?"

Then Jesus tells them the ultimate, objective truth. "I am the Way, the Truth and the Life. No one comes to the Father except through me." Jesus is not only the path to the Father's house. He is not just the one who provides us with abundant, eternal life. Jesus himself is the truth! What he said, what he did, his very nature, is the truth.

We know there are plenty of people in the world who don't believe in Jesus, are sure God does not exist, and think the Bible is no more than a collection of stories about how to live right. They are staking their life on Jesus not being who he says he is. That is not a risk I am willing to take.

Jesus is the truth. We can trust him.

The Truth Came Out – Peck Music Publishing

2 Corinthians 5:21

A breastplate of armor covers your chest. It protects your heart and your lungs, two key things that keep you alive. You can live with one kidney or without an arm or a leg. You're fine with only part of your liver or intestines. Doctors can remove your spleen or appendix, and you will be alright. But if they remove your heart or lungs, you're done.

So, this breastplate of righteousness is obviously an important part of our armor. Before we move on to righteousness and how we get it, we are going to define a word that might be new to many of us. 'Impute', in a financial sense, means to credit an account. For example, at the end of the month, your bank account is credited with the interest you have earned. That money was the banks', now it's yours. We usually hear imputed in a legal sense, to impute a sentence. You did this wrong, and to pay your debt, you will do this or that. The responsibility for this crime and the payment of the debt is laid on, or imputed, to the person who did the crime.

I realize it is unusual for us to look at only one verse. This is a simple verse that tells us about a profound truth. Let's break it down.

'For our sake.' If I do something for your sake, it is to benefit you, often at my own expense. Because you are breaking, for your sake, I will pay for your groceries.

'He made him to be sin who knew no sin.' Who are the 'he and him'? 'He' is God the Father, and 'him' is Jesus. Jesus lived here on earth with no sin. He went to the cross as the innocent, perfect Son of God. While Jesus was there, God imputed our sin onto Jesus. Jesus became responsible for the crime of our sin and the payment of the sentence of death, because the wages of sin are death. Romans 6:23

'So that in him.' 'Him' is still Jesus. When we believe in Jesus and have faith that his death on the cross is our salvation… when we abide in him and surrender our lives to him, God does something very special.

'We might become the righteousness of God.' Our belief in his Son causes God to impute to us his own righteousness! His righteousness is credited to us because of our faith. It's a double imputation! Our sin is given to Jesus, and His righteousness is given to us. Amazing!

Now, when you are buckling on your breastplate of righteousness, remember that Jesus is your righteousness. He will guard your heart.

His Robes for Mine – Hymns of Grace, Hymnology

Other resources: Merriam-Webster Dictionary: Impute

John Piper, 'Faith and the Imputation of Righteousness'

1 Corinthians 15:1-5/Colossians 1:19-23

You've possibly been there. I have. Everyone slept in. You're running late to get everyone to school. They have already missed the bus, so you are driving them to school. You've been after them all morning, "Eat your breakfast, fast! Get dressed, brush your teeth! Do you have your shop project? Get your baritone sax in the car! What do you mean, where's my backpack?!"

You're throwing the last things in their lunches and yell around the corner, "Are you ready to go?"

They answer in unison, "Yes!"

Thirty seconds later, you come around the corner and lose the last bit of composure you had.

"GET YOUR SHOES ON!!"

Ephesians 6:15 tells us that the armor of God for our feet is the 'readiness given by the gospel of peace.' So even Jesus knows we're not ready to go if we don't have our shoes on!

What is this gospel of peace? In 1 Corinthians 15:1, Paul reminds the Corinthian church that they are standing in the gospel he preached to them. This is what he preached, which was of first importance:

1. Christ died for our sins, just like the scriptures told us he would. Verse 3

2. He was buried

3. He was raised on the third day, just like the Scriptures said he would be. Verse 4

4. He appeared to many. Verses 5-8

Those are the basics. Each point can, of course, be filled out as we learn more about what and why we believe, but these four things we must believe and stand on. No wavering.

Paul calls it the Gospel of peace. What does that mean? Colossians 1:19-23 make it quite clear:

1. Jesus was fully man and fully God. We may not understand it fully, but we must trust it. Verse 19

2. Jesus reconciled us to himself. 'Reconciled' means we have peace and a relationship with God, and it only comes through Jesus' death on the cross. Verse 20

3. We were alienated from God because of our hostile minds and deeds. Verse 21

4. Jesus' act of reconciliation means he can present us to God as holy and blameless. Verse 22

5. IF we continue in the faith, standing with stability and steadfastness.

There you have it. The outline for the gospel of peace. You can take that outline and fill it in with your own testimony at the appropriate spots. The bottom line, though, is that Jesus is the gospel of peace! Get your shoes on and be ready to go!

I Believe – Phil Wickham

Hebrews 12:1-2

Arrows are an interesting weapon. They are quiet. One little bow twang and a whistle you don't hear until it is right there. It's a stealthy weapon. The archer can be in hiding until the moment he chooses to release an arrow on an unsuspecting victim. A volley of arrows can be used as cover or a distraction for a much bigger, more lethal weapon. In battle, they would be a constant hinderance. If I am in a swordfight, I need to be focused on my combatant, not worrying about arrows.

An arrow is a tool for a targeted attack to inflict harm on a specific person. And according to Ephesians 6:16, the evil one, aka Satan, has a whole slew of them. And he's smart with them. He will choose arrows specifically for you and me, knowing just where our weaknesses are. On top of that, he lights them on fire. An arrow that is on fire will not only harm you worse than an unlit one, but it can start things around you burning, even if it misses.

To deal with Satan's arrows, Paul tells us to always keep our shield on hand in every circumstance. We never know when those arrows are coming. And this shield has a superpower! Not only can it deflect arrows, but it can extinguish the fire on the lit ones! Kapow!

What is our superpower shield made of? Faith.

The definition of Faith is 'the assurance of things hoped for and the conviction of things not seen' Hebrews 11:1. It is trust in Jesus, the salvation he provides and knowing that he will be who he says he is and do what he says he will do.

To use our shield, we need to look at Hebrews 12:1-2. This is the instruction label on the back.

FOR BEST RESULTS:

- Lay aside extra weight. Trust Jesus to take the heavy things.
- Lay aside sin. Have your breastplate of righteousness securely in place.
- Run with endurance.
- Keep your eyes on Jesus.

This Shield Manufactured by:

Jesus

The Founder and Perfector of your faith

When I was a girl, I memorized this verse in the King James Version, which says Jesus is the Author and Finisher of our faith. He wrote the book and will complete the work of building our faith himself. As you may have figured out by now, Jesus is our Shield of Faith.

Faith is the Victory – Josh Snodgrass

Faith is the Victory

Encamped along the hills of light,
Ye Christian soldiers rise
And press the battle ere the night
Shall veil the glowing skies
Against the foe in vales below
Let all our strength be hurled
Faith is the victory, we know,
That overcomes the world

Refrain: Faith is the victory
Faith is the victory
Oh, glorious victory
That overcomes the world

His banner over us is love,
Our sword the Word of God
We tread the road the saints above
With shouts of triumph trod
By faith they, like a whirlwind's breath
Swept over every field
The faith by which they conquered death
Is still our shining shield?

To him that overcomes the foe
White raiment shall be given
Before the angels he shall know
His name confessed in heaven
Then onward from the hills of light
Our hearts with love aflame
We'll vanquish all the hosts of night
In Jesus' conquering name

John H. Yates 1837-1900
Ira D. Sankey, 1840-1908

Acts 4:1-22

Peter and John, not long after being given the Holy Spirit, have just, through faith in Jesus, healed a lame beggar who had sat at the Beautiful Gate for years. Everyone seemed to know who he was. He was over forty years old, so he had been there for as long as some could remember. This man is walking and leaping and praising God!! (3:8) and it causes quite a stir. Since Peter had his gospel of peace shoes on, he stood up and gave a sermon, and 5000 men were saved that day!

The Sadducees, who did not believe in the resurrection from the dead (which is what made them sad, you see!), were annoyed. They arrest Peter and John, put them in jail overnight and gather everyone to examine them in the morning. They have the rulers, the elders, the scribes, Annas, the high priest, Caiphas, John and Alexander and the high priests' family. This was not a small gathering; there would have been dozens of men there, along with many curious onlookers. You may recognize some of the names; they were among those who plotted to have Jesus crucified only a few weeks before. These people hate Jesus and anything to do with him.

They ask Peter and John about the man who had been healed, "By what power or by what name did you do this?"

Peter lays it on the line. Guided by the Holy Spirit, he tells these men the bold, raw truth. Imagine Peter, in the middle of this group of men, projecting his voice so everyone can hear. Now read verses 8-12 like Peter would have said them.

No pulled punches there:

This was done in the <u>name</u> and power of <u>Jesus Christ.</u>

<u>You</u> crucified him.

<u>God</u> raised him from the dead.

<u>You</u> are supposed to be the builders of God's Kingdom.

<u>You</u> rejected <u>the Cornerstone.</u>

'And there is salvation in no one else, for there is no other name under heaven given among men by which we can be saved." Verse 12

Paul tells us to put on our helmet of salvation:

Your good works can't save you.

Your parents' relationship with Jesus can't save you.

Going to church every Sunday for 50 years can't save you.

Doing all the religious actions you are told to do can't save you.

Trying to be a good person can't save you.

No other religious system can save you.

The only thing that saves you from death in your sin is believing and accepting Jesus's saving work by his death on the cross and repenting from your sin. Your salvation comes in Jesus' name only.

Jesus is your helmet of salvation.

Name of Jesus – Chris Tomlin, Lyric Video

Deuteronomy 4:6-9/John 1:1-18

The sword of the Spirit, the word of God, is the only offensive weapon included in the armor of God. All the other pieces are defensive. When Jesus was being tempted after his forty days in the wilderness, he didn't give Satan long explanations about why he was rejecting Satan's offers. It was one verse answers, straight out of the Scriptures. Matthew 4:1-11

The logical progression then, is that if the Bible is our only weapon against the rulers, authorities and cosmic powers of this world, we had better be saturated with it! How do we do this? Deuteronomy 4:6-9 is a good blueprint. The word of God is to be:

- On our hearts

- Passed on in our families

- Spoken in every situation.

- A sign that they are following God

- A signature on your home that God rules and reigns there.

So, dig in, memorize it and learn it. Let it be the central theme of your prayer and daily life. It is crucial to protect yourself from Satan's schemes to pull you away from Jesus Christ and into his world.

The other way we saturate ourselves is to stay close to Jesus. How is that? It is outlined in John 1:1-18.

'In the beginning' is also how the book of Genesis starts. So, whoever John is talking about here was present at creation.

'Was the Word, and the Word was with God and the Word was God.' So, this Word was present at creation, and the Word is also God.

Okay, this sounds really confusing. How can someone be with someone and also be the someone? It straightens out if you have a grasp on the Triune God. In Genesis 1:2, it also speaks of the Spirit of God. So, we have God, the Word, and the Spirit of God all present at creation. They are all equally God, yet have distinctive roles. The Trinity is a big theological concept to wrap our heads around.

John 1:14 says, "The Word became flesh and dwelt among us, and we have seen his glory, glory as of the only Son from the Father, full of grace and truth." Ahh, the pieces are coming together. The Word is the Son of God! Jesus Christ is the Word of God. He is the living representation of God and has made God known to us.

If the Sword of the Spirit is the Word of God, we must saturate our lives with the scriptures and abide in Jesus Christ, the living Word of God.

Jesus is the Sword of the Spirit!

My Weapon – Natalie Grant, Sacred Version

Romans 13:11-14

There are occasions in our lives when we all need to change our clothes, besides the regular everyday reasons. You don't wear your dirty, stained work clothes to a wedding. You don't wear your bathing suit to a courtroom. You wouldn't wear a tuxedo or ball gown to go camping in the mountains. It would be foolish to walk into a war zone in your everyday clothes.

In case you didn't quite pick up the common thread while we were looking at the armor of God, it's Jesus!! He is our truth, our righteousness, our gospel of peace, the founder of our faith, our salvation and our sword.

In Romans 13:11-14, Paul first tells us that it's time to wake up, because Jesus is coming back soon! Our salvation from this world is nearer than we first believed. If Paul felt the nearness of Christ gathering his church to himself, how much closer is it 2000 years later? If the night was pretty much gone and morning was on the edge of dawning, the Son is starting to peek over the horizon now! The church's time to be with Jesus could be any moment, so it's time to wake up and get dressed!

'So cast off the works of darkness.' Verse 12. Take off sexual immorality, quarrelling and jealousy. Remember that Paul is writing to believers here. If you need further lists of sinful things to cast off, there are plenty. Try Galatians 5:19-21, 1 Peter 4:1-5, 2 Corinthians 12:20, Ephesians 4:25-31, Romans 1:29-32.

After we cast off all the evil things, it's time to get dressed. We can't go into battle unclothed. 'So put on the armor of light. Verse 12.

And in verse 14, Paul says, "Put on Jesus Christ…' We need to clothe ourselves with him.

Jesus is our armor.

Honestly, We Just Need Jesus – Terrian, Official Music Video

Isaiah 1:1-20

Have you ever seen (or been?) a child who obeys their parents on the outside, but it's obvious they are not obeying on the inside?

The one sitting in the time-out chair and glaring at the parent who put them there. Or the kid in the back seat of the car who has been told to leave his sister alone, but has one finger half an inch away from her arm, saying on repeat, "I'm not touching you!" I may have raised that child, and I may have been that sister, too!

The child is technically obeying what they were told to do, but there is defiance in their heart. They don't really want to stop what they are doing wrong, so they go as close to the edge as they can.

Judah had pushed God as far as they could. They were doing all of the sacrifices, just as God had commanded through Moses, but their hearts were rebellious and sick, corrupt and estranged, despising God and refusing to recognize Him. Vs 1-6

The sacrifices at the temple were intended for Israel to be a symbol of repentance and ongoing faithfulness and love toward God. Those are all heart issues. So, when the outward actions were not reflecting the inward truth of the people, God used Isaiah to say, "Enough!! Just stop all of this. It is detestable to Me." Vs 7-14

What did God want from them?

For them to do good, seek justice and stop oppression.

Help the most vulnerable.

To clean their bloody hands and their evil hearts and then come to the Lord and pray. Vs 15-18

God, like any good parent, finishes this very hard talk with, "If you do this…I will do this. But if you choose to do this…then this will happen instead." Vs 19&20

If there is one person we can trust to follow through on what He says will happen, it's God.

Are you doing all the 'right things' to look good, but your heart isn't right with God? Obedience in your actions only has real value, in God's eyes, if it matches what is in your heart.

Clean Heart – Bryan and Katie Torwalt

Daniel 7:9-28

The only place where the term 'Ancient of Days' shows up in scripture is here in Daniel 7. Daniel is having a vision about the end times, and he sees the Most Holy on His throne. As with all of God's names and titles in the Bible, this one means something, so let's unpack it a bit.

The setting here is that of a courtroom vs. 10. You might have noticed that there were thrones, plural, placed, but there is only one Ancient of Days. The other is for 'one like the son of man, coming in the clouds of heaven' vs 13. Any time in the Bible where you see a statement about 'the son of man coming in the clouds of heaven', that is Jesus.

Therefore, the first characteristic we can ascribe to God with this special name is that of being the ultimate, righteous Judge. He is the only one who can judge in both spiritual and earthly realms.

We see that He has one million serving Him and one hundred million standing before Him. I doubt Daniel counted them all…the point is, there were innumerable beings in His service and before His throne. The Ancient of Days has the authority to command as many as come to Him. He also has the authority to give Jesus all dominion, all glory and a kingdom. Vs 13&14. This God is almighty, and there is none over Him.

This kingdom he bestows on Jesus and then to his people, is an everlasting dominion that shall not pass away and cannot be destroyed, vs 14 & 27. This Ancient of Days is an everlasting, eternal God. And if He is eternal into the future, he is eternal into the past. He is the God who created the heavens and the earth with a word.

He is omniscient, omnipresent, omnipotent and immutable.

Quick translation: He knows everything, He is everywhere, He is all-powerful, and he does not change.

The Ancient of Days is worthy of all worship, all praise and all glory.

P.S. (Pre-Song) As a bass player, the first time I saw this, my mind was a bit blown. If I have to audition with this guy for a spot on heavens' worship team, I will obviously be in the choir and not playing bass! This song is longer than most, but it is joyful worship of the Most High, the Ancient of Days!!

Ancient of Days – Integrity Music Live, Ron Kenoly

Titus 3:1-7

I don't really like caterpillars. I don't like how they look, how they move or that they eat green, pretty things. I do like butterflies. My Mother-in-Law has a small butterfly collage in her dining room. The colors are gorgeous. The structure of the wings and the way some are naturally designed to camouflage themselves is amazing.

When a caterpillar cocoons itself to become a butterfly, a process called metamorphosis occurs. The caterpillar releases enzymes that essentially digest itself, ending up as goop inside the cocoon. In the goop are cells called imaginal discs that have encoded in them the information to take the goop and restructure it into a butterfly.

Now, we could talk about God's amazing imagination when he created caterpillars that could turn into slime, and the slime becomes a butterfly (Mind-blown emoji here). Or we could refute evolution by explaining a closed system requiring all of the parts to fully function so that any of it could work (yes, I said that out loud!). But we don't have time for that discussion.

Let's talk instead about becoming a new creation.

We start out as distasteful caterpillars. According to verses 2 & 3, we are foolish, disobedient, slaves to our own passions, full of hatred, envy and malice.

Now, I don't understand the details of how the whole thing works, and I don't think we can fully grasp it this side of heaven, but Paul says in 2 Corinthians 5:17, "Therefore, if anyone is in Christ, he is a new creation. The old has passed away; behold, the new has come."

Verses 4 & 5 in our passage help us know how this happens. When the goodness and loving kindness of Jesus come to us, he saves us. Nothing we have done contributes to that; it's because He is merciful. Then the Holy Spirit washes us, regenerates and renews us.

I know what you're thinking, because I am thinking the same thing. If I am saved, washed, regenerated and renewed, this new creation, why do I still struggle with sin? Paul had the same problem.

Romans 7:14-25 probably contains several sermons, but let me try to make it as concise as I can. Paul, in the previous verses, is talking about the law, sin and righteousness.

Verse 14: The law is spiritual, but the flesh is still sinful.

Verse 15: Paul doesn't understand his own actions (just like us!) He wants to do the right things, but instead does what he hates.

Verse 17: It's not me who is the problem, but the sin that is still within me. (Exactly, Shonnon. The sin is still there, so how can I be a new creation? Stick with me...and Paul)

Verses 18-23: Paul knows what is right and has the desire to do it, but not the ability to do it, because nothing good dwells in the flesh. Paul says it is a consistent thing (a law) that whenever he wants to do what is right, evil is right there, ready to mess it up. He feels like he is at war with himself!

Verses 24 & 25a: Who will deliver me from this body of death? God, through Jesus, will!

Verse 25b: So then, I serve the law of God with my mind, but with my flesh I serve the law of sin.

So, our minds and our hearts are washed and renewed by the Holy Spirit, but we are still stuck living in the same flesh as we did before that happened.

I hope that brings some understanding of how caterpillars become butterflies in God's kingdom. One day, soon, we will be changed and have new bodies, leaving the sinful flesh behind (1 Corinthians 15:51). That will be a good day!

P.S. You can listen to the whole song if you wish, but listen at least halfway!

Oh, What a Day – 2002 Stamps Baxter School of Gospel Music

Other Resources: Scientificamerican.com, August 10, 2024, 'How Does a Caterpillar Turn into a Butterfly?'

Psalm 51

My son and his best buddy used to get into all kinds of trouble. They would often build projects or try things that weren't the safest, but somehow, they both survived into adulthood.

We had moved to a different house and were renovating the old one, so we took the living room carpet out of the old and put it in the basement of the new, temporarily, so the kids didn't have to sit on the concrete. When the boys were about 11 or 12, they came to me one day and asked if they could take the carpet out of the basement. It was old and moved around as they were playing, and they couldn't build stuff on it.

It seemed a bit fishy to me, and I reminded them that getting it out with all the furniture on it would be really hard work. They said it was no problem, and they really wanted to do it. I agreed and let them go at it. A couple of hours later, the carpet was rolled up beside the garbage can, the furniture was back in place, and nothing was broken.

Several years later, they admitted that they had burnt a hole in the carpet.

They had hidden the evidence of their arson attempt. They came up with a plausible excuse, put in a lot of hard work, and no longer had a carpet to sit on in the basement.

A burnt carpet and murdering the husband of your mistress are two very different kinds of sin. However, the process was the same.

David saw Bathsheba and got her pregnant, and he devised a plan to make it look like the baby was her husband's. When that didn't work, David revised the plan and made sure that Uriah (her husband) was killed in battle. Then he brings Bathsheba to his palace, and it looks like her pregnancy is legitimate. Nice cover-up. Until the prophet Nathan calls him out.

David now has adultery, murder, and deception in his heart. His trusted advisors know everything. The baby boy dies, just as Nathan prophesied. David's dream of building a beautiful temple for the God he loves and worships is taken away.

And he pens **Psalm 51**.

Are there things you need to put before the Lord? Listen to "Create in Me a Clean Heart" and lay it all out. He will forgive, renew, and restore your heart.

Create in Me a Clean Heart – Keith Green

Genesis 16

There is a young woman I know who is talented, a great mom, loves the Lord, and has a smile that welcomes people into her life.

She also has older siblings who are equally as talented but are more outgoing, with stronger personalities that can overwhelm hers. Even when she has a great idea, or can do something as well, or better, than them, she can get trampled in their dust, or disregarded entirely. Just getting a word in edgewise can be a challenge for her when they are around.

I sat down beside her one day when I knew she was discouraged and told her that I could see her. It was what she needed to hear. Someone knows. Someone cares. Someone sees me.

Hagar had fled from Sarai and Abram. Abram didn't seem to care much about what happened to her or his own unborn baby. Sarai was jealous that Hagar had become pregnant so easily and was angry with everyone around her, and probably herself for coming up with the idea of giving Hagar to Abram in the first place.

Hagar finally had to leave. As she was sitting by the spring, the Lord came to her, and she realized she had been seen by God. Despite her situation, God saw her. Though she had been arrogant about her pregnancy, God saw her. When people didn't seem to care or overwhelmed her with their position or personality, God saw her. Over in chapter 21, when she is again under attack from a jealous Sarah, God sees her and takes care of her.

Hagar gives God one of His names: El-Roi, The God Who Sees

Psalm 33:13&18 tell us that the Lord looks down on us from heaven and sees all of us. That sounds distant, but if you read verse 18, it is much more personal:

"Behold, the eye of the Lord is on those who fear him, on those whose hope is in His steadfast love."

Today, remember that El-Roi sees you, loves you and knows you.

El Roi/ The Elohim Who Sees Me - A Song of Comfort /English-Hebrew Messianic Worship

John 17:1-13

Have you ever noticed how often Jesus tells the people around him that his hour or time hadn't come yet?

In John 2:1-12, he is at a wedding in Cana, and his mom asks him to solve a lack of wine problem. Jesus says, "It's not my time yet." Vs 4. The implication here is that the time for him to be revealed in his ministry role isn't quite there yet. In typical Mom-fashion, Mary tells the servants to just do what he tells them. Can you see Jesus shaking his head and smiling at Mary? I'm sure he checked in with his Heavenly Father and then did what Mom asked.

Luke 4:16-30 is early in Jesus' ministry. Jesus has read a passage from Isaiah and essentially told them he is the Messiah they are expecting. Verse 28 says the people were 'filled with wrath'. So they took him to throw him off a cliff. Somehow their eyes were blinded, and Jesus calmly walked away through the crowd. It wasn't his time yet.

In John 7:6 & 8, Jesus repeats to his family that his time isn't here yet. His teaching had made the Jewish leadership angry enough to plot to kill him, and Jesus implied it wasn't his time to die. Jesus goes to the feast anyway, and there he teaches more things that make the leadership even more angry. By verse 32, they are trying to arrest him, but they can't. It's not time yet.

In John 8:20, they try to arrest him again, but his hour had not come yet.

Finally, after three years of ministry, Jesus tells his disciples, "It's time." They head to Jerusalem for the Passover and the last few days of Jesus life here on earth. John 13:1

In John 17:1, after a long talk with his disciples, he prays and says, "Father, the hour has come…" This prayer is often called his High Priestly Prayer. Jesus prays that he will glorify his Father, the Father will glorify him and that all who follow him will forever be in his hand, kept secure by the Father.

Jesus' most critical hour on earth was his death, so he could pay the price for our sin, and his resurrection, to overcome death and offer us eternal life in him.

2 Corinthians 6:2. Paul quotes Isaiah 49:8 and says:

"'In a favorable time, I listened to you, and in a day of salvation I have helped you.' Behold, now is the favorable time; Behold, now is the day of salvation."

Jesus needed to wait for just the right hour, but for us, the time to be with him is right now.

Now is the Time – Evie, Mirror

P.S. It took me a long time to hunt this song down! Apparently, the internet wasn't around in 1977.

Psalm 99

Canadians have a speech quirk where we will double a word to express an extreme of something. For example, "It's cold, cold." That's not for a -10 Celsius degree day in the winter. That is -35 Celsius with a wind chill of -47. It feels like it cuts through your coat and will actually give you frostbite on exposed skin in one or two minutes. (Yes, those are real temperatures!) We do the same with lots of other words as well, like 'hot hot' or 'mess mess'.

Interestingly, it is a speech habit we share with the Hebrew language, and they will go up to three repeats! So, if you say to a friend, "We had a storm," - they might reply with, "Well, the garden got a good watering."

If you say, "We had a storm storm!" - they might say, "Oh no, did your house get flooded?"

But if you say, "We had a storm storm storm!!" - they will start asking questions in a panic. "Are you and the kids okay? Is your house still standing? Do you need a place to stay?" Three 'storm's is a devastating, hurricane-type storm.

There are three places in the Bible where 'Holy' is repeated three times. Isaiah 6:3 is when Isaiah is given a vision of heaven. He sees the Lord, and the angels are repeating, "Holy, holy, holy is the Lord of Hosts. The whole earth is full of his glory." In Revelation 4:8, John is taken to heaven in the Spirit, and the angels are saying, "Holy, holy, holy is the Lord God Almighty, who was and is and is to come." In both cases, it is the angels proclaiming God's supreme, extreme, overall holiness. Maybe they understand it better in God's presence than we do in our humanness. For

Isaiah, it brought him to his knees in worship and in understanding of the depth of his own sin.

David, in Psalm 99, also proclaims God as holy three times, though not all together like the angels do. In verses 3 and 5, "Holy is He!" is the cry. And at the very end, he adds, "The Lord our God is holy."

What should our response be to the holy, holy holiness of God? Like Isaiah, we need to recognize who we are in the light of His holiness. David gives us ways to respond:

- V 1 God reigns, and we tremble. He sits enthroned, and the earth quakes

- V 2 God is great and exalted

- V 3 So we praise His awesome and great name

- V 4 He loves justice, establishes equity and executes justice and righteousness

- V 5 So we exalt him and worship at his footstool

- V 6-7 God answers those who call to him. We call on him and obey what he tells us

- V 8 God forgives, but also avenges wrongdoing

- V 9 So we exalt him and worship at his holy mountain

We can not proclaim God as holy, and then move on like it doesn't matter. His holiness demands a response of worship.

Holy, Holy, Holy – David Andrews, Album: Hymns

Lyrics are on the following page

Holy, Holy, Holy

Holy, holy, holy Lord God Almighty

Early in the morning my song shall rise to thee

Holy, holy, holy merciful and mighty

God in three persons, blessed trinity

Holy, holy, holy! All the saints adore Thee

Casting down their golden crowns around the glassy sea

Cherubim and seraphim falling down before thee

Which wert and art and evermore shall be

Holy, holy, holy, Lord God Almighty

All thy works shall praise thy name in earth and sky and sea

Holy, holy, holy, merciful and mighty

God in three persons, blessed trinity

By Reginald Heber and John Dykes

Copyright 1861, Reginald Heber and John Dykes

Psalm 104

Do you have a favorite spot where you love to go because the glory of God's creation is almost overwhelming? Maybe it's in the mountains, or a quiet spot by a lake. Perhaps it's in your backyard with the perfection, detail and beauty of each flower. For me, it's the ocean. The vastness, power and mystery simply astonish me. When I am near the ocean, I am drawn to it and can't help but praise God for the beauty He created for us to enjoy! Sadly, I don't swim well, and I am fearful of deep water, so I have never mustered enough courage to go snorkelling. Maybe that's my next personal growth project!

This Psalm reminds us that we really have little to do with how our planet functions. God provides the water for the plants and trees. God provides the water, food, hiding places and homes for the animals. God provides the sun and moon to mark the seasons. The parts and pieces of this world that we have learned to use, cultivate and enjoy…He created every molecule.

Now, I am going to move a bit away from standard theology here and share what I was thinking while reading. Verse 29 says something interesting. In talking about how God provides for the animals, the psalmist says, "When you hide your face, they are dismayed." I don't think animals have souls, because God breathed our souls into us at creation, and did not do that for animals. And I don't know how much self-awareness animals have. But I somehow think that they are aware that they are created by God and recognize that what they need is provided by Him. After all, if a donkey can see and tell Baalam about the angel blocking the pathway (Numbers 22:22-33), and ravens feed Elijah (1 Kings 17:1-7) and a large fish can swallow Jonah and puke him out on shore on God's command (Jonah 1:17, 2:10), there must be something going on with the creatures!!

The only response we can have to the wonder of God's creation is to praise him as the Creator and Sustainer of it all!!

May the glory of the Lord endure forever; may the Lord rejoice in His works. V.31

I will sing to the Lord as long as I live. I will sing praise to my God while I have been. V.33

Bless the Lord, O my soul! Praise the Lord! V. 35

God of Wonders – Caedmon's Call

Psalm 107

We all have times when we are in distress. It is a normal part of life. What do we do when the circumstances around us or our own foolishness bring us into distress? This Psalm gives us guidance on how to deal with times of overwhelming distress.

We start by remembering that God is good and he loves us. We testify about how he has redeemed us and reached into our lives before.

We meet four groups of people in this Psalm. The first are lost, lonely and poor. They cry out to God, and he delivers them from their distress. He leads them to a city to live in and fills their empty hearts. And they thank Him for His goodness.

The second group is rebels who are in chains, surrounded by darkness and death. They are imprisoned because they have spurned God and his council. God disciplines them until they cry out to Him, and he delivers them from their distress. He rescues them from darkness and death and frees them! God bursts the bonds, shatters the bronze doors and cuts apart the iron! What a picture of release! They must thank him for his goodness.

The next group we meet is fools trapped in their own sin. They refuse the good things God provides for them until they are almost beyond hope. Then they cry to the Lord, and He delivers them and heals them. They need to offer sacrifices of thanksgiving and tell of His deeds with joy!

Our final group is out on the sea doing business. Not so bad, except they are not giving any mindfulness to God. So, God makes them pay attention! Their courage is gone, they can't stand up straight, they are seasick, and they finally reach their 'wit's end', so as a last resort…you know what happens…they cry out to the Lord, and He delivers them from their distress. The storm and the seas are quiet, and they need to testify to God's goodness.

If you are lost, bound in chains, trapped in sin you brought on yourself or ignoring the Lord, this is a good time to cry out to the Lord so He can deliver you.

And then remember to thank Him for his goodness and tell others what He has done.

The Goodness of God – Live - Cece Winans

Ezekiel 1

Take a moment and think about how you would describe the taste of a strawberry to someone who had never had one.

Or imagine trying to describe penguins and where they live to a person who has lived in the Sahara Desert their whole life. It's a bird, but its body is like… and it has wings that are like… but it can't fly, so it swims and it lives on what are like mountains of water that are so cold it is hard, like a rock, and the water rock looks like…" They would think you were crazy!

Now you are getting a bit of the feeling that Ezekiel must have had trying to write down what he had seen. He needed this to make some sense to the people who were going to read it, but how do you describe the indescribable to people who hadn't seen the same thing you had seen?

We always filter what is new through what we already know, so poor Ezekiel is trying to tell his readers what Almighty God's throne room looks like, and what God himself looks like, and what the angels and beings that attend to God look like, by using word pictures of things they are familiar with. There is a lot of

'It was like…'

'…had the likeness of…'

'As it were…' (we would say 'It was as if it were…')

'…had the appearance of…'

You get the sense that what Ezekiel wrote couldn't quite describe in completeness what he had seen.

He finishes his description with "Such was the appearance of the likeness of the glory of the Lord. And when I saw it, I fell on my face…" vs 28.

Would there really be any other response? He was so overwhelmed that when the Lord told Ezekiel to stand so He could speak to him, the Holy Spirit had to lift him to his feet. Ez 2:1 & 2

What would my response be if I saw the Lord in all his glory? Pure, unadulterated worship is the only response.

Glorious – Chris Tomlin

Revelation 21 & 22

I was going to have you read a portion of these two chapters, but they really do belong as a whole, and once you start reading them, you don't really want to stop!

Your favorite verses here might be different than mine. I love chapter 22:3-5. The throne of God and the Lamb and all who serve Him will be there. We will see his face and be marked by him as his own possession. God will be the light and we will worship him forever.

Look how many names there are for Jesus in these chapters;

- 21:6 - The Alpha and Omega

- The Beginning and the End

- 21:9 – The Lamb

- 22:6 - The God of the spirits of the prophets

- 22:13 – The First and the Last

- 22:16 – the Root

- The Descendant of David

- The Bright Morning Star

    So many reasons to worship Him!

I also love how 22:17 is an invitation to "Come." The invitation has been placed and the time to come to Jesus to accept the gift of eternal life in Him is now. Things here can be hard, and we sometimes forget to look ahead to the joy of heaven when we are dealing with here and now. Remind yourself today that what you see now is not all there is.

These chapters are the culmination of it all. God has dealt with sin and death and evil. Everything that was corrupted has been destroyed. The Lamb has overcome. God has brought all of his people home and made everything new!

Rev 22:20 He who testifies to these things says, "Surely I am coming soon." Who is that? Go all the way back to the beginning of Revelation 1. Verses 1and 2 tell us that this is the revelation of <u>Jesus Christ</u>. John bore witness, but the testimony is from Jesus!

Amen. Come, Lord Jesus

I've Read the Back of the Book – The Cathedrals

1 Corinthians 15:1-4, 50-58

There is a simple tool that can be used to teach children the gospel. Sometimes it is just a few pieces of construction paper cut into shapes. You can find it in books or pamphlets. When I was a children's ministry director, one of my vacation bible school kits had a glove with different coloured fingers.

Black was our sin

Red was Jesus' blood shed for us on the cross

White was how our hearts are clean when we come to Jesus

Green was our new, growing life in Christ

Gold was our hope of heaven

The beauty of the gospel is that it is so simple a child can understand it, yet theologians can study it for their entire lives and not fully comprehend the depth and breadth of God's plan, His love and His sacrifice.

Paul says in verse 3 that the death, burial and resurrection of Jesus were the most important teaching he gave them. This is what saves them, what they stand in and what they must cling to. Vs 1&2. So, verses 1-4 cover the black, red and white fingers on our glove. We are sinful to the core. Jesus' death, burial and resurrection save us. When we believe in Jesus, he cleanses and purifies us.

The middle section of this chapter addresses how Christ's resurrection and ours are connected, and that without His resurrection, there is no point in believing what we believe.

Verses 50-58 talk about our last two colours.

Verses 56-58 are the green finger on our glove. We have new life in Christ! He gives us victory over sin. We can be steadfast and immovable in what we believe. And we can confidently do the work the Lord wants us to do.

Verses 50-55 remind us of our hope of heaven. Jesus is coming back, and we will be changed and go to be with him!

Simple. Clear. Straightforward. So, if you need some guidance to share the gospel with someone, remember:

Black, Red, White, Green and Gold

It's About the Cross - The Ball Brothers (Yes, this is a Christmas song – sort of!)

John 12:1-8/Matthew 26:6-13

The day before Jesus' triumphal entry into Jerusalem, and six days before his crucifixion, Jesus was in Bethany. He was having dinner with his disciples at Simon, the leper's house, and Lazarus, Martha and Mary were hosting.

Lazarus was reclining at the table with the disciples. Martha, as usual, was serving, John 12:2. Martha sometimes gets a negative light thrown toward her, but I think I understand what she was doing. When my mom is hosting a dinner, she is always busy! It's hard to get her to sit down long enough to eat! It's one of the ways she shows us she loves us. For Martha, this was a very practical way for her to show Jesus and the disciples that she loved them.

Then Mary comes in. She kneels before Jesus, and in an act of extravagant worship, she pours a full pound of expensive nard on Jesus' feet and head. Then, after anointing him, she wipes his feet with her hair. Some of the disciples were indignant, thinking it was a waste, but Jesus stopped that immediately and reminded them that he would not be with them much longer. He accepts and justifies Mary's act of worship.

Are there ways you can extravagantly worship Jesus? There may be something the Holy Spirit has been prompting you to do, but you have avoided it because you fear what other people will say or think. Maybe it's as simple as raising your hands in worship this Sunday, when you have never done it before. Perhaps it's a financial gift for someone in Jesus' name. Or he may be asking you to use your musical gifts to lead in worship when you would rather not be on stage.

Jesus is our Saviour, Redeemer and King. He deserves our most extravagant worship.

The Great Exchange/The Girl Who Broke the Alabaster Jar – Sarah Liberman – The Invitation Version. Please watch the video of this song.

P.S. A few days after I wrote this, my worship leader called me on Saturday afternoon. She was sick. Could I take the team and lead worship tomorrow morning? "Sure!!" Inside, I was quietly panicking.

I have been on stage for years as a musician, but I have not led for at least 18 years. Time to stretch out of my comfort zone! Then I went back and read this. Who says God doesn't have a sense of humor

Psalm 115:2-8/Isaiah 46:1-7

There are several places in the scriptures where God compares idols to Himself. Let's do a brief comparison:

- The nations have gods they can see (Psalm 115:2).
- Our God is in the heavens and does as He pleases. (Psalm 115:3)

- Their idols are silver and gold, formed by human hands (Psalm 115:4).
- Our God knits us together in the womb and knows us intimately (Psalm 139:13-16).

- Their gods have mouths but do not speak (Psalm 115:5).
- Our God has spoken through His word, and it shall never pass away (Matthew 24:35).

- Their gods have eyes but do not see (Psalm 115:5).
- Our God sees and knows our hearts (1 Samuel 16:7, Psalm 139:1-3).

- Their gods have ears but cannot hear (Psalm 115:6).
- Our God hears us when we cry to Him (Psalm 145:19, 1 Peter 3:12).

- Their idols have noses, but do not smell (Psalm 115:6)
- Our God accepts our prayer as incense (Psalm 141:2)

- Their idols have hands but do not feel (Psalm 115:7).
- Our God has engraved His beloved ones on His palm (Isaiah 49:16).

- Jesus laid his hands on people to heal and bless them (Matt 8:2-3, Mark 10:13-16)

- Their idols have feet but do not walk (Psalm 115:7).

- Our God is omnipresent (everywhere, all at the same time) (Psalm 139:7-12).

- Their idols need to be carried around by livestock (Isaiah 46:1-2).

- Our God carries us from the womb until we are old and gray. He made us, so He will bear us (Isaiah 46:3-4).

Our God is Living, All-Powerful, All-Knowing, the King of Kings, the Lord of Lords. He alone deserves all of our worship.

You Are God Alone - Phillips, Craig & Dean

Psalm 116

In my fourth year of Bible College, I was part of a music team that travelled. There were nine of us, our director and a speaker from the school, so eleven, in a 15-passenger van for a 10-week tour. You get to know each other very well.

One of our team members, Richard, was a few years older than most of us. He was proudly from Lunenburg, Nova Scotia and had a Ty Beanie Baby Lobster given to him from someone special back home named 'Lobbie'. Richard was incredibly intelligent, had a quirky sense of humor and loved the Lord with his whole heart.

After graduating, he went on to become a missionary with Wycliffe Bible Translators to the people in Guyana who spoke the Wapishana language. From 1994 until Spring 2005, he and his wife, Charlene, rented a farm among the people they loved and continued translating the Bible into their language.

At the end of March 2005, Richard's body was found burned, and Charlene had been bludgeoned to death. The authorities came to the conclusion that it was a robbery, but only God knows the motives of the people who did this to my friend and his wife.

Psalm 116 is about how our bodies die, but God will save our souls.

Vs 3&4 – Death was near, and the psalmist asks the Lord to deliver his soul.

Vs 7 – Reminds us that God has been good, so my soul can return to rest.

Vs 8&9 – Talk about the 'land of the living'. That sounds a lot like the paradise Jesus talked about. None of us escape death here on earth, but our souls can be delivered from death.

I love verse 10 – "I believed, even when I spoke, 'I am greatly afflicted.'" Hold on to your faith, even when it's time to meet the Lord.

Verse 16 – 'Precious in the sight of the Lord is the death of His saints." 'Precious' seems to be a strange word to use in conjunction with death, but God knows that is when our soul returns to His presence.

What a comfort it is to know that when it is time for our bodies to die, God is right there to gather our souls in his arms and carry us home. When Richard and Charlene were in pain and afraid, Jesus was right there with them. They saw their murderers one moment and the Lord they had faithfully served the next!

Are you ready for that moment, however and whenever it comes? Is Jesus your Saviour, your Lord, and your Friend? Now is the time to make sure you are ready to be gathered into his arms.

Hymn of Heaven – Phil Wickham

Other resources: CBC News, Nova Scotia, 'Missionaries Killed in Guyana', April 5, 2005

Psalm 119:105-112

Back in the olden days, before we all had Google Maps on our phones (2008!), our daughter was 16 and off on her first mini road trip by herself. She was going to a city 2.5 hours away from home for a band camp and staying overnight with a friend who lived about half an hour further away.

Before she left, we thought we had given her very clear instructions on how to get around the city and swing back onto the #1 Highway. Unfortunately, when I said "Ring Road turns on to Victoria," she understood that "Ring Road turns into Victoria," so she just kept going. It's an understandable mistake.

After hours of no contact, we got a phone call. She was very lost and diagonally across the city from where she was supposed to be.

When I asked her how she got there, she said, "I was following a guy in a black truck. He looked like he knew where he was going."

I replied, "I'm sure he did know where he was going, but he didn't know where you were going!"

We broke out the paper map and directed her back to where she needed to be, so all was well.

We know the end goal as Christians; we are supposed to follow Christ and look more like him all the time. If you aren't in your Bible and listening to solid, reliable teaching from trustworthy people, it can be easy to end up somewhere you never intended to be.

Paul says in Acts 17:10-12 that the Bereans examined the scriptures daily to see if what Paul and Silas were teaching them was correct. They received the truth, confirmed that it was true, and then believed.

Don't just trust that the guy in the black truck knows the truth. He may confidently be going completely the wrong way and lead you off to a place that is the opposite of where God wants you. Get in the word yourself and confirm that it's true. If you aren't sure, look at it with a trusted fellow believer. Pray that the Holy Spirit will show you the truth through the word.

We are so blessed to have the Word of God in our hands. It's our map to get us to where we are intending to go, and it will light the way in front of us. But it can't do that if we don't use it. Dig in, read it, explore it, love it, and obey it.

Thy Word - Amy Grant

John 14:15-31

We had a worship leader in one of our churches who would often begin his worship package with "Standing on the Promises". Every time he did, he would say, "Folks, you can't sing 'Standing on the Promises' while you're sitting on the premises, so rise and let's sing together!" It's funny the first few times, obviously memorable, and it endeared him to the congregation.

Did you notice, when you read the passage, how many times the word 'will' is used? Seventeen times in sixteen verses! In this one short passage, there are sixteen promises that Jesus gives us of what he, the Father and the Holy Spirit <u>will</u> do.

Jesus promises us the Holy Spirit.

Jesus promises not to leave us, that he will come to us.

Jesus promises the Father loves us.

Jesus promises that because he lives, we will also live.

Jesus promises the Holy Spirit will teach us.

Jesus promises us his peace.

Now, because Jesus is the Way, the Truth and the Life (14:6), we can take what he says and know it is a solid foundation to build our lives on. We can trust what he says.

So, when you read your Bible, watch for things that Jesus says he will do. Those are solid promises you can stand on!

Standing on the Promise – The Georgia Mass Choir, Jaqueline Saunders, Savoy Records Inc.

3 John

One evening, while on a college music tour, the person at the church who coordinated our being there forgot that we needed billets for the night. They found enough people with enough beds to house us all, and off we went. It was quite normal for our hosts to be exceptionally hospitable. "Here's your room, there's the washroom, would you like a cup of tea, do you need a snack, tell us where you're from…." And so on.

The lady my friend and I were sent home with obviously did not want company that night. The car ride to her house was silent. We were ushered to a room in the basement with no invitation to emerge. My friend, who was much bolder than I, asked if we could get something to drink, and the lady begrudgingly brought us a tray with two glasses of water, two spoons and a container of iced tea mix. As we stirred our beverage, I noticed little larvae carcasses floating in my glass and decided I wasn't that thirsty after all. My friend said, "Well, down the hatch!" and swallowed her glass of buggy iced tea in one long gulp. In the morning, there was no invitation for breakfast, no lunch sent with us, and I have never been so glad to get out of a fellow-believer's house!

I don't know what was going on in her life when we interrupted whatever she was dealing with, but I have often wished I had given her some sort of encouragement. However, it was a very good lesson for me. Like everyone, I like to have things in place when company comes, but sometimes you just have to take the unfolded laundry off the couch and be hospitable!

John is writing his letter to Gaius, and the first thing he notes is how kind the church is to fellow Christians, and they are walking in the truth, except this one guy. Diotrephes is a real

175

problem. He will not recognize the authority of the apostles. He will not welcome people into their fellowship, and if others want to, he will try to kick them out of the church! I can't imagine a church putting up with that!

Then John points out Demetrius. Everyone respects and loves him, and he is recognized as a godly man. Is John hinting that it is time to put Demetrius in charge and put Diotrephes in his place, perhaps outside the door? It is in this context that we find this verse:

"Beloved, do not imitate evil but imitate good. Whoever does good is from God; whoever does evil has not seen God."

We all have people we look up to and imitate; be careful who you choose! Choose people who are like Demetrius. They are wise, kind and hospitable. They love the Lord and his word. They put into practice what the word tells them and live in a way that pleases God,

My friends, the people around you can tell very quickly who you are living for. Are you living for yourself, or God? Become a person living for God that others want to imitate.

Take My Life – Chris Tomlin

Matthew 6:1-18

Jesus says three things in this passage, three times each. The first is "that they can be seen by others." The second is, 'They have received their reward", and the third, "Your Father who sees in secret will reward you."

He uses the examples of giving to the poor, praying and fasting. The people who are doing religious things for public show, he calls hypocrites. Most of us have a good idea of what a hypocrite is: it is someone who says one thing, but their actions oppose what they say they believe. Jesus makes it very clear that when people put on a display of their religion so that other people will see it and praise them, it is from a selfish, sinful heart. Their status here and the praise of people are more important to them than their reward in God's kingdom and His approval. They already have their reward.

Jesus goes on to say, with each example, to do these things privately. Just give, without any fanfare. Just pray, you and your Father, simply and honestly. Just fast, without any outward display, it's just between you and God.

As a musician, I struggled for a long time with how to do this. God gave me a voice that is pleasing to the ear, and when I use it for His glory, I am often complimented. How do I do 'in secret' something that is so public?

You've probably seen sports figures who, when they score the points and the crowd roars, will point to the sky. It is a sign of the praise they are receiving being deflected to God. Essentially, they are saying that God gave me the ability to do this, so praise him, not me. For years, I tried to do something similar. I would say things like, 'God gave it to me' or try to explain that the 'performance wasn't a performance, it was supposed to be ministry'. Somehow, it just didn't feel like people were understanding.

I have learned some things over the years.

First, I have learned to make sure, in my heart, that I am doing this to honor my Lord.

Second, I have learned that most people just want to acknowledge that they enjoyed it, so a simple 'thank you' is all that is needed.

Third, if a person heard something from God through what I did, I have the opportunity to listen, encourage and pray with them. That is where the real ministry happens!

And fourth, I have learned to look for other opportunities to minister in secret to those around me.

So how do we manage the desire that many of us have for the praise of men?

First, hate hypocrisy. Don't let it get a foothold in your own heart and gently call it out in Christians around you.

Second, don't place value in petty, fleeting rewards. You sang great last Sunday, and everyone loved it. This week, you hit some wrong notes, and no one said anything. Are you crushed? Then your focus is too much on the rewards people give you.

Third, remember that your Father sees your heart, and his rewards for glorifying him in what you do are so much deeper, richer and more gracious than anything offered by those around you.

My Reward – (Official Lyric Video) – Simply Worship and Austin Ludwig

Matthew 6:25-34

On the surface, Jesus makes not being anxious sound so simple: 'God will take care of you, so seek after Him and don't worry.'

Jesus has just been talking about laying up our treasures in heaven. Devote your life to things that have eternal value. Then in verse 24, he reminds us that we can't serve God when we are focused on gathering money and possessions for ourselves.

Now, let's take what Jesus is saying with a realistic point of view. Jesus is **not** saying:

Don't bother working.

You should expect to dress like Solomon.

Don't concern yourself with the needs of your family.

Don't plan for your future.

Go ahead and spend what you have on whatever you want.

What he is saying, though, is that God, your heavenly Father, has things taken care of. If he feeds little birds and makes the flowers in the meadow beautiful, he will take care of you, too.

Jesus tells us in verse 30 that the main reason we worry about things has to do with our faith. If our faith is so small that we are anxious about things we can do nothing about, like how long we are going to live, we need to start growing our faith.

If our faith is so small that we can't believe our Heavenly Father loves us enough to make sure our needs are met, then we need to start growing our faith.

How can you do that?

Keep your eyes open. Watch for the small ways God intervenes in your life everyday. Be conscious of the unlikely things that just seem to happen at the right time, and recognize that God is in control.

Be thankful for everything. When you start to remember all that God has blessed you with in the past, it gradually becomes easier to remember that He has tomorrow in his hand as well.

Trust your heavenly Father. If he has done it before, he can do it again.

While you are doing what your daily life requires, remember whose kingdom you are a part of. Seek to represent your Father by how you live and work. If, or when, things get down to nothing, continue to be grateful for what is left in the pantry and closet, then trust God to take care of what you need for tomorrow. There are days when you only have enough faith to deal with today. So, deal with today, in faith; then give tomorrow to your Heavenly Father, in faith.

A Million Ways – Sanctus Real, Unstoppable God

Psalm 121

I love the "Songs of Ascent" from Psalm 120-134. Most of them are only a few verses long, so the point of each one is usually clear. And they tend to be joyful!! These were the songs the Israelites would sing together as they were going to Jerusalem for the feasts. Jerusalem is on a mountain, so they literally had to ascend the hills. They would sing to encourage each other on the way up and to express their joy in going to the city Jehovah had claimed for his own.

I think most people appreciate knowing that someone is looking out for them. A toddler in a new setting will start to explore, all the while checking back to make sure Mom or Dad is watching. A gymnast doesn't tackle a difficult move without a spotter. NASCAR drivers have spotters high up over the track who can see what is going on ahead of them, always in communication, especially if there is a problem!

As the people were looking up to Jerusalem on the hills ahead of them, the question they ask is 'Where does my help come from?' The short answer is 'My help comes from the Lord, the maker of heaven and earth!'

Almighty God, the Creator, is my helper! He is the one looking after me!

He is called my keeper in the rest of the psalm. Let's look at how he keeps us.

He will not let your foot be moved. It's that sense of standing on something solid.

The God who keeps Israel does not sleep or slumber. Our God watches us night and day. He doesn't need rest as we do, and regardless of when you need him, he is always ready.

The Lord is our shade. When you are walking up a hill in the hot sun, nothing feels better than a shady spot. Sometimes, things just get difficult. Life starts coming at you too fast and too hard. God promises to be your refuge and refreshment.

The Lord keeps us from all evil. He protects us, often even when we don't realize we need protecting.

He will keep your life. There is just nowhere safer we can be than living under his care.

He will keep you going in and you're going out, now and forever. It doesn't matter where you are, he is there. There is no one more reliable that you could have looking out for you.

God is not far away, just making sure the universe is functioning, not thinking about us at all. He is a personal, loving Father who will always keep us close. He loves us, and that will never change.

P.S. The song sung by Birgitta is in Hebrew. The words are in your Bible, Psalm 121

Song of Ascents – Birgitta Veksler

Psalm 124

We have a small ski resort just a couple of hours from home in the Cypress Hills. We're not talking Rocky Mountain skiing, but it's entertaining for a day and a great place for beginners to learn. At least that's what I was told.

Another family, who all ski, invited us out to spend the day with them. I had never skied before, so my friend, Pam, stayed on the bunny hill with me for a while, teaching me the basics. I was not really picking it up well, so I told her to go enjoy herself, and I would keep practicing. After a good hour and a half, I could finally make it down the very gentle slope without falling. So, I decided to try my hand at Bunny Hill Two.

Now, Bunny Hill Two might look pretty straightforward to most people, but I could not master it. My skis would get crossed, and I would fall down. I would lose my balance and fall down. I would try to do the side-to-side thing and fall down. I would try to stop and... you get the picture.

The last time I went down the hill, I didn't fall down!! However, I was unable to control the direction I was going and ended up off the side of the hill by the trees, tangled in a snow fence.

If I couldn't go forward on skis, how was I supposed to go backwards up the slope and get pointed in the right direction? I was definitely in trouble. Suddenly, I feel someone grab the back of my coat and pull me backwards out of the fence. It was our friend John, who had come to check on me at just the right moment.

I expressed my appreciation for saving me from the snow fence and assured everyone this would not happen again. My attempt at skiing was over, and I went to the lodge to enjoy some hot chocolate and a magazine.

In this song of ascents, the people recognize that if the Lord had not been on their side, they would have perished. The anger of their enemies had overwhelmed them like a flood that sweeps everything away in its path. (vs. 4-5)

But the Lord did not allow that to happen. He rescued them from the snare, and they have escaped!! He pulled them out of the snow fence and set them on solid ground.

We all get trapped in a spiritual snow fence every now and then. But God is good, all the time, and He will break the snare and pull you free. Remember who your help comes from: The Lord who made heaven and earth!

God is on My Side - The Jackson Southernairs

Mark 4:35-41

Jesus had a long day. If you look at the preceding verses in Mark and in the coordinating passage in Matthew 8, he had spent the day teaching and healing, and he was tired. He asks the disciples to get the boat, and they head over to the other side of the Sea of Galilee. Jesus falls asleep not long after they set out.

While He is catching a nap, a storm comes up and threatens to sink the boat. Finally, after trying to save themselves, they wake up their sleeping Master and ask him why he doesn't seem to care that they are all about to die! Then Jesus rebukes the wind. He told the wind to just stop. And he says to the sea, "Peace, be still."

The wind stopped, and the sea was calm.

Out of curiosity, I decided to do a small-scale experiment. I put about 2 inches of water in my bathtub and made waves with my hand. When I took my hand out of the water, I started my stopwatch, and it took just over 4 minutes until there was no perceptible motion in the water. If you are on the Sea of Galilee, which is much bigger and deeper than my bathtub, and you are in a storm with waves big enough to swamp the boat, even after the wind stops, it will take quite some time for the waves to settle down.

Unless you are with Jesus, and he tells the sea to be calm. Then it happens immediately, and that is not what seas do. The disciples were terrified, more than when the storm was about to sink them. It was early enough in Jesus' ministry that perhaps they did not quite yet understand who he was. They had seen him heal and do other miracles, but some of these men were fishermen; they knew how bodies of water behave, and this was not normal. The wind and the waves had all just stopped.

Jesus asks the disciples why they are so afraid. Do they not yet have enough faith to know that when they are with him, they are safe? Do you still not understand who I am, that you are fearful when I can control what I created? You have seen me heal and cast out demons. You have heard me teach, but you still don't have enough faith to believe that I am the Son of God?

I asked someone recently to tell me about a couple of milestones in their spiritual walk that helped build their faith. Both of the things they told me were scary experiences that would have overwhelmed them, but Jesus pulled them through. Now I ask you, do you have a couple of storms you can look back on and say, "Jesus was right there. He did a miracle, and it helped me believe him and love him more.?"

Jesus Calms the Storm - The Getty Girls, Keith and Kristyn Getty

1 John 3:19-24

After a period of time struggling with the aftermath of a sin I deeply regretted, I felt utterly defeated. I had asked God for forgiveness. I knew in my head that he had forgiven me, but in my heart, I just couldn't let it go.

One day in the midst of it, I came across these verses, and they started me on the path of restoring my relationship with God and myself. My heart had definitely been in a cycle of self-condemnation. If I were a better Christian, I wouldn't have done that. How can God forgive me when I just can't seem to move forward, and I am stuck here in my guilt? I try to do the right things and say the right things, but I feel like a failure in my walk with God.

So, when I read, 'By this we shall know that we are of the truth and reassure our heart before Him..."

I thought, "That's exactly what I need. My heart needs to be reassured that he has forgiven me and that he still loves me."

Verse 20: '...for whenever our heart condemns us...'

Yes, that's me!

'...God is greater than my heart, and He knows everything.'

God is greater than my sin.

He is greater than my guilt.

He is greater than my self-condemnation.

He is greater than my sorrow.

He knows what I feel.

He knows that I have begged for forgiveness.

He knows how I have tried to fix it on my own.

He knows exactly what I need to feel whole again.

C.S. Lewis said, "I think that if God forgives us, we must forgive ourselves. Otherwise, it is almost like setting ourselves as a higher tribunal than Him."

It sounds ridiculous that my heart would decide it can't be forgiven and free when the God of the universe has given me forgiveness and freedom.

Now, by no means am I saying that you should turn off your conscience. Verse 21 tells us that if our hearts are clean, we know that we have confidence before God. The Holy Spirit uses that feeling of guilt and shame to tell us that something is not right. It's a reminder to keep ourselves abiding in Christ and keep a clean account with the Lord. But we aren't supposed to stay there. When forgiveness has been sought and given, we repent and move forward in our relationship with Christ.

This doesn't necessarily happen overnight; our human habits are hard to break. But if you continue to go to your Father, trusting that he is greater than your heart, that he loves you and forgives you, even when he knows everything, your self-condemnation will eventually ease.

Greater Than Our Hearts – Tim Mottershead, Official Lyric Video

Other resources: C.S. Lewis, 'Collected Letters of C.S. Lewis'

Deuteronomy 1:19-46

Israel had been wandering around in the desert for 40 years, and it's now time to go into the land. The bulk of Deuteronomy is Moses's last words of leadership before they go in, and the first thing he does is remind them that they could have been in the land God gave them 38 years ago if they had just listened to God and Moses in the first place.

So, what happened to leave Israel in the great and terrifying wilderness?

First, they were hesitant. Moses took them to the edge of the land and said, "There it is, now go get it." And the people said, "Let's send in a few guys to scope it out…"

Not the worst idea, but God had spent two years preparing them and promising to be with them. The spies came back with reports of really good land and really big people.

Second, they are now fearful, and that fear causes grumbling, murmuring and a bit of whining. All God has done for them is forgotten, and He has now become the enemy. "God hated us so much that he brought us here through the great and terrifying wilderness, just so we could be destroyed by the people of this land."

Third, the fear causes them to rebel. They simply refuse to go. God has had enough, and he sends them back into the wilderness.

When the people discover there are consequences to their actions, they now regret their decision. Suddenly, they have all the courage in the world and decide to obey God's command, but it's too late. God has made his judgment. He will not go with them.

They rebel against the word of the Lord again and go fight the people without him. And, of course, they lose the battle miserably. Now they come before God and cry out, but he has turned away and will not listen.

There is a verse in the middle of the passage that unlocks the whole process of how the people reacted to being at the edge of the land and refusing to move ahead.

Verse 32: "Yet, in spite of this word, you did not believe the Lord your God."

God miraculously brought them out of Egypt, destroyed their enemies and provided them with food. He faithfully led them to places to camp with his own presence. And they still would not believe Him.

Not believing God leads to hesitancy, fear, rebellion, grumbling, sorrow, presumptuousness and self-effort. If we would just believe, trust and obey, the road ahead may be hard, but it will always be victorious, and God will always be with us.

Are there things God is asking you to do and you are thinking, "I don't know, let's analyse this some more"? It might be the first step down a long road away from the good things God has ready for you.

God Will Make a Way – Acapella Praise, Hosanna Music

Ecclesiastes 3:9-15

My favorite fairy tale as a child was 'The Elves and the Shoemaker'. The shoemaker is in debt, he and his wife are out of food, and there is only enough leather to make one more pair of shoes. He lays the leather on his workbench and decides that tomorrow he will make the last pair of shoes and sell them. After that, they will be homeless and starve to death.

Overnight, the elves show up and make an exquisite pair of shoes from the leather on the workbench. The man is, of course, shocked but grateful. He sells the shoes for double what he normally would, goes out and buys more leather for the next day. Of course, the elves return, and the pattern continues. The shoemaker and his wife start to leave little gifts for the elves. They keep coming back, and eventually, the shoemaker is the wealthiest man in town, making shoes for the king!

The saddest part about growing up is discovering there are no elves. No elves come to pick up your toys or tidy your room. No elves come to do your math homework or clean the bathroom. No elves come to do your taxes or put the dishes in the dishwasher. The moral of the story is no longer, 'Good things happen to good people.' Now it's 'You are responsible for your own stuff, so get on with it."

God has given us the job of staying busy. Even in Eden, Adam was tasked with caring for the garden and the animals. So, Solomon, in a rare moment of encouragement in this book, tells us that one of the best things we can do with our lives is to do good, eat, drink, be joyful and take pleasure in our work. It is God's gift to us.

Sometimes our work may seem pointless. The dishes keep getting dirty, the laundry hamper keeps refilling, and the paperwork at your job is never-ending. But keep at it and remember that God gave it to you for His purpose.

Now, look at the contrast of God's work. It becomes beautiful when he plans for it to be beautiful. His work is eternal. His work is complete; neither does he need to add to or take anything away from it. What has been driven away, he will restore. And he does it all so we will fear him and worship him.

So, whatever you do, whether word or deed, do everything in the name of the Lord Jesus Christ, giving thanks to God the Father through him. Colossians 3:17

My Story, Your Glory – Matthew West, Official Music Video

Luke 4:16-21/Isaiah 61

Jesus reads a part of his job description in the Nazareth synagogue and finishes with the statement, "Today this has been fulfilled in your hearing." His ministry is just underway, and he proclaims in his hometown; This scripture is about me. This is what I am here for.

These people had watched Jesus grow up. He was the weird kid who never got into any mischief, did too well in the classes at school and always had the right answer. So when he tells them he is the Messiah, they are offended and try to kill him. Luke 4:29-30

Perhaps they were too angry to notice where he stopped in the Isaiah passage. He is proclaiming good news, liberty, recovery and the year of the Lord. It reminds me of the conversation with Nicodemus. In John 3:17, Jesus says about himself, "For God did not send his son into the world to condemn the world, but in order that the world might be saved through him." Jesus came the first time to seek and to save the lost.

So, what is the rest of the job description, and why didn't Jesus read that part?

The last part of Isaiah 61:2 says he is also proclaiming 'the day of vengeance of our God.' There is a lot packed into that phrase. This is also referred to as the 'Day of the Lord' in the Bible and is a time of judgment on the world for those who rebel and refuse to follow Jesus. The next time Jesus comes to stand on the earth, he will be returning as Judge.

After that, he will be our comfort and joy. Many will be mourning, but he will give them gladness and strength.

Remember that Jesus isn't just a gentle Shepherd to his people. He is also the King of Kings and Lord of Lords and a Righteous Judge. When it is time, righteousness and praise will grow before all nations because Jesus will be King!

The King in All His Beauty – Sovereign Grace Music

Lamentations 3:17-32

Jeremiah is sometimes referred to as 'The Weeping Prophet', so a book written by him, named Lamentations, makes some sense. This book of five poems was likely written shortly after the fall of Jerusalem to Babylon when they destroyed the city. Jeremiah's laments come from a deep passion for God's righteousness, God's people and God's city.

Then, tucked right in the middle of the sorrow is the basis of one of the most dearly loved songs in recent church history: Great is Thy Faithfulness.

Jeremiah's soul is broken and bowed because of the despair he sees around him, but there is one thing that gives him hope!

In spite of all that is around us:

God's love and mercy never end. They never run short; every morning, there is just as much as there was yesterday.

The <u>Lord</u> is our inheritance, not all of the things around us that have been destroyed.

God is still good to those who seek him.

God's punishment for the unrighteousness of his people will end, because he is compassionate.

Are you in a time of mourning in your life? Regardless of what the loss is, you can call this to mind and find some hope. Hope doesn't mean the loss, the destruction or the pain go away. It means that in spite of all of those things, you <u>know</u> that God loves you, he is merciful and compassionate and faithful. So, at the end of the tunnel, there is a light, because God is good.

Great is Thy Faithfulness – Worship Refocus, Vocal Arrangement

Psalm 146

You've probably seen a 'trust fall' or done one yourself. Someone stands on a chair or something, crosses their arms over their chest, closes their eyes and falls backwards. Meanwhile, 3 or 4 people are there to catch them, maybe. What if something distracts them? What if they aren't strong enough? What if they don't like me and decide not to catch me? It is against our instinct to deliberately fall backwards off of something, so the faller must trust that the catchers are going to hold up their end of the bargain.

Sometimes it's easy to misplace our trust. Our human instincts tell us to trust what we can see, what looks like it has power, and the things that are supposed to be stable. But in verse 3, the psalmist tells us not to misplace our trust in people or government or people who appear to have power. They have no power to save you. They make plans for good or not, but when they die, all their plans die with them.

Then the Psalmist reminds us who is worthy of our trust. We have the Lord, who keeps faith forever, executes justice, upholds the weak and ruins the plans of the wicked! What's more, He is eternal, and when he dies, he is raised back to life! His word and plans are solid. He will reign forever!

I would be willing to fall into the arms of an eternal, righteous, living God who loves me! Praise the Lord!

Faithful Now – Vertical Worship

Ephesians 1:3-9

Sometimes Pauls' sentences make my head hurt! Paul is notorious for writing long sentences that seem to never end, and it's easy to read a passage like this and miss all of the richness in it. Halfway through, you have forgotten what the point was and just start reading words without putting together what they mean.

We're going to do something different today and break down part of this passage grammatically so we can extract all the points that Paul has in his writing. Once you see how it's done, you can take sentences that make your head hurt and break them down to see what the author is really talking about! Something to note: don't go by verse numbers. Not a single author in the Bible used chapter and verse numbers! They were added later. Use the sentences.

Blessed be the God and Father of Jesus Christ,

> who has blessed us with every spiritual blessing
>
> > in the heavenly places,
> >
> > > even as He (God the Father) chose us in Him (Jesus Christ)
> > > before the foundation of the world,
> > >
> > > > that we should be holy and blameless
> > > >
> > > > before Him (God the Father).

So, we are breaking the long sentence into shorter ones:

Blessed be the God and Father of Jesus Christ.

Blessed be the God who has blessed us with every spiritual blessing

Blessed be the God who has blessed us in the heavenly places

Blessed be the God, even as he chose us.

Blessed be the God, even as he chose us in him (Jesus Christ).

Blessed be the God, even as he chose us before the foundation of the world.

Blessed be the God, even as he chose us that we should be holy.

Blessed be the God, even as he chose us that we should be blameless before Him (God).

When you do this, you start to see the details of the passage, and really learn how it applies to you. I also find it helpful to note in parentheses who the pronouns belong to so I can sort out who did what to whom. Let's look at the next sentences.

In love, he (God) predestined us

    For adoption as sons

    Through Jesus Christ

    According to the purpose of his (Gods') will

    To the praise of his glorious grace

With which he (God) had blessed us in the Beloved (Jesus)

In Him (Jesus) we have

    Redemption through his blood

    The forgiveness of our trespasses

    The richness of his grace

    Which he (Jesus) lavished upon us

    In all wisdom and insight

    The knowledge of the mystery of his will

    According to his (Gods') purpose

    Which he (God) set forth in Christ

As a plan for the fullness of time
To unite all things in him (Jesus)
In heaven
And in earth

What stood out to me as I looked through this? He chose me to bring him praise and glory. He has made the mystery of his will known to me through Jesus. One day, heaven and earth will be united under Jesus Christ, our Redeemer! If you have time, try the next sentence yourself. (Verses 11-12)

Adoption Song – Brandon Lake, Lyric Video

James 1:19-25

Over my whole life of being in church almost every Sunday, I have heard hundreds of sermons. Add to that, four years of Bible College with daily chapels… It's a lot. There are very few sermons that I can specifically recall, but there are some that stood out. One in particular, though I can't remember the speaker, I remember exactly what he spoke on. James 1:22-25, looking in the mirror and doing nothing about the problems you see. Why do I remember that one, and not other sermons on exactly the same passage? Because he played Michael Jackson's 'Man in the Mirror' to open his sermon! Quite a surprise at a very conservative Bible College in the '80's!!

James tells us that if we hear the word of God and do nothing about it, we are deceiving ourselves. This person is going to church on Sunday because he feels he needs to do his duty to God, and then shelves his Christianity for the week. It doesn't affect his day-to-day life at all. The self-deception happens because he thinks he is doing what is required. 'I showed up, I wore the right clothes, I sang the songs, I listened to the sermon. God can't expect much more of me than that, I am a busy person.' Did they even really take a good look in the mirror?

Verses 23-24 tell us about the person who looks in the mirror of God's word and sees where they need to make changes. There is spinach in between their teeth, their hair is unruly, and there is dried ketchup on their chin. Then they shrug and walk away like it doesn't matter.

So, if you read verses 19 and 20 and the Holy Spirit nudges your soul about how you sometimes get angry without knowing the whole situation, you can start learning to control your anger, or you can ignore the Holy Spirit's prompting and just keep snapping at people, for what are really just minor inconveniences.

But the one who looks into the perfect law of God's word, perseveres and acts on what it says, is blessed, and it brings liberty.

Pay attention, wash the ketchup off your chin and change what God is asking you to change!

Word of God Speak – Mercy Me

1 Corinthians 5

One of the ladies I worked with in the dining hall at Bible College was from Germany. English was her second language, and sometimes she sounded quite abrupt. She was not a person to show a great deal of emotion. She was in her late forties, maybe into her fifties, and I confess, she scared me a little!

Feeding 1100 students three meals a day was a daunting task, so we would do all of the prep a day ahead and everything would be ready to cook. This lady was getting about 40 pounds of vegetables prepped for sweet and sour pork, all into a couple of bins, ready to dump in the kettle when it was time. I was in the office entering inventory into the computer. Suddenly, I hear a scream from the kitchen!

I ran out of the office to find her backed up against a counter, wide-eyed, uttering a string of German words that I don't think were Christ-like. Of course, I went and asked if she was okay. She shook her head and pointed to the bin of veggies. Tucked in amongst the pineapple chunks she had just poured in was a complete five-inch-long praying mantis. He had managed to get into the fruit before it was canned and scared the bejeebers out of my coworkers.

She asked if I thought she would have to re-prep all of the vegetables now. I knew the answer, but suggested that she ask our head cook what she thought. I really just wanted her away from the situation so she could calm down.

I carefully wrapped the offending creature in plastic wrap and placed him and the can label on the manager's desk so he could appropriately deal with it after his meeting. The veggies were thrown away and re-prepped.

All of that to say a small thing can cause big problems. Just like a little bit of yeast leavens all of the bread and a little (or not so little) bug can waste a lot of food, a single person in a body of believers can corrupt that church. The sin must be dealt with, or it can spread and ruin the body and their testimony.

It also applies to us as individuals. Just like the yeast causes all of the dough to rise; that one area of sin in our heart we want to hang on to, to not repent of, can lead to compromise in many more areas of our lives. Christ died for us as a sacrifice so we can be cleansed and new. He loves you, and he wants you to clean out things that can cause bigger problems for you. Bring it to him and let him renew you.

Refiners' Fire – Brian Doerksen, It's Time

Proverbs 16:20-33

One of the students who was on the music team I coached was an adorable young lady with bouncy blonde curls, big brown eyes and the prettiest smile you can imagine. We all loved her. There was a spirit of innocence about her, and she approached her faith and the world around her with a joy and freshness that was infectious. She sometimes didn't think about what she was going to say before it came out of her mouth. She would occasionally ask a question to which the answer was obvious, or make a statement in a way that made you think she had just come up with a brand-new idea (that most of us had figured out before!)

Once on a music trip, she was sitting at the back of the van, and our very competent driver was reversing with a trailer attached. She suddenly starts shouting, "You're fork-knifing, you're fork-knifing!!" All of us, including her, laughed until we cried. I still can't see a jack-knifed truck and trailer without thinking about it as having fork-knifed…

Our passage today is all about how we need to think about what we say before we say it. Wise people are considerate, discerning, have good sense and are self-controlled. A paraphrase of verse 23; a wise person thinks before they speak, so their words are more effective.

Verse 32 says that if you can control your spirit, you have more strength than a person who overthrows a city, especially if you are dealing with a conflict or disagreement. Don't let your emotions get control of your tongue. Slow down, get your emotions under control and then trust the Lord and ask for discernment.

Give thought to your words. Ask yourself, 'Can I say this with graciousness?'

The wisdom God gives us shows up in what we say. And in what we don't say.

Words – Hawk Nelson, Official Lyric Video

Luke 14:25-33

Count the Cost – David Meece (Listen now, I know this is a departure from our regular format!)

One of the main things I have been learning as I have been writing is that our relationship with God is a two-way street. God offers forgiveness; we have to confess and repent to have it applied. Jesus offers us eternal life; we need to abide in him. The Holy Spirit grows fruit in our lives; we need to keep in step with him. God promises peace; we need to be still and understand who he is. He promises blessings; we need to obey. The list goes on.

Luke records for us that Jesus said we need to make sure we consider the cost of being his disciple. I don't think he meant that you have to actually hate your family, but your love for him needs to be so much more than your love for them that you would be willing to give up those relationships for his sake. We all know the stories of people who come to Jesus, and their family rejects them. It would be a high price.

He says there is a cross to bear.

He says to make sure you can complete the job. Christians who had a great start and then give up on their faith cause unbelievers around them to say, "I knew he couldn't follow through."

"Yeah, it was just a crutch for a hard part in their life." "I guess Jesus isn't as powerful as she said. She's worse off now than she was before."

I wonder if, as believers, we don't make it sound too easy sometimes. 'Jesus changed me. Jesus carries me. Jesus will make your life so much better. You need Jesus.' But there is more to it than that. Jesus can and will do all those things. Our part is renouncing our old ways, not clinging to the world, walking with Him, carrying whatever cross he gives us to bear. Knowing that pleasing him, not the people around us, is the best way.

Salvation is through faith in Jesus' work on the cross. Period. I am not adding anything to that. What I am saying is the surrender of our hearts to him as Saviour, Master, King and Lord requires everything we have. It is not a once-and-done prayer, and then I go on with my life. It's a day-to-day relationship with Jesus that affects everything we do, what we say, how we think and all of the decisions we make.

Jesus didn't promise that being his disciple would be easy. In fact, he said it would be difficult. And he promised that if we do what we must, it will be worth it.

Worth It All – Brooklyn Tabernacle Choir.

Index

Passages in Biblical Order to Song Titles

Passage/verses	Song title	Artist	Further Documentation
Genesis 1:2	My Weapon	Natalie Grant	Sacred version
Genesis 4:1-16	Acceptable to You	Calvin Institute of Christian Worship	Friday, July 24, 2020
Genesis 16	El-Roi - The Elohim that Sees	Timeless Hebrew Tunes	
Genesis 29:9-29	Patience	The Music Machine	
Genesis 29:9-29	Yes, I Will	Vertical Worship	Bright Faith, Bold Future
Genesis 48:15-16	Lead Me To The Rock	Christourlife	
Genesis 49:22-26	Lead Me To The Rock	Christourlife	
Exodus 12:1-28	Oh Praise the Name (Anastasis)	Shane and Shane	Live
Exodus 14:15-16	How Majestic is Your Name	Sandi Patti	
Leviticus 19:18	Lord, Shine Your Light	Elevation Gospel Worship	2004
Deuteronomy 1:19-46	God Will Make A Way	Accapella Praise	Hosanna Music

Deuteronomy 4:6-9	My Weapon	Natalie Grant	Sacred version
Joshua 22	Build Your Kingdom Here	Rend Collective	
1 Samuel 16:7	You Are God Alone	Philips, Craig and Dean	
1 Samuel 17:1-49	Voice of Truth	Casting Crowns	New York Sessions
1 Samuel 17:34-54	The Battle Belongs	Phil Wickham	
2 Samuel 21:15-22	The Battle Belongs	Phil Wickham	
1Chronicles 28:9	Nothing Else + The Heart of Worship	Kari Jobe	
Job 38	Wonderful Peace	Fourhope	
Psalm 4	Endless Hallelujah	Matt Redman	
Psalm 8	How Majestic is Your Name	Sandi Patti	
Psalm 9	Adore and Tremble	Daniel Renstrom	
Psalm 10	Lord Of All	Kristian Stanfill	
Psalm 16:11	Endless Hallelujah	Matt Redman	
Psalm 19	Here's My Heart	Casting Crowns	Official Live Performance
Psalm 19:14	The Rock Won't Move	Vertical Worship	

Psalm 20	He Will Hold Me Fast	Selah	
Psalm 23	Psalm 23	Phil Wickham, Tiffany Hudson	
Psalm 25	While I'm Waiting	John Waller	
Psalm 27:1-14	Patience	The Music Machine	
Psalm 27:1-14	Yes, I Will	Vertical Worship	Bright Faith, Bold Future
Psalm 33:13	El-Roi - The Elohim that Sees	Timeless Hebrew Tunes	
Psalm 33:18	El-Roi - The Elohim that Sees	Timeless Hebrew Tunes	
Psalm 37	Step By Step	Rich Mullins	
Psalm 40	Part the Waters	Evie	
Psalm 40:1	Patience	The Music Machine	
Psalm 40:1	Yes, I Will	Vertical Worship	Bright Faith, Bold Future
Psalm 42	We Come	Keith Kitchen	
Psalm 44:22	The Promise	The Martins	
Psalm 46	Be Still and Know	Steven Curtis Chapman	Instrumental Worship Ensemble

Psalm 47	Clap Your Hands	Shane and Shane	Kingdom Kids
Psalm 49	Blessed	Vertical Worship	
Psalm 51	Create in Me A Clean Heart	Keith Green	
Psalm 51:12	Endless Hallelujah	Matt Redman	
Psalm 61	Lead Me To The Rock	Christourlife	
Psalm 66	How Great Thou Art	Peaceful Piano Version	Paul Hankinson Covers
Psalm 95:1	The Rock Won't Move	Vertical Worship	
Psalm 96	Symphony of Praise	Steve Green	Live
Psalm 99	Holy, Holy, Holy	David Andrew	Album, 'Hymns'
Psalm 104	God Of Wonders	Caedmon's Call	
Psalm 107	The Goodness of God	CeCe Winans	Live
Psalm 115:2-8	You Are God Alone	Philips, Craig and Dean	
Psalm 116	Hymn of Heaven	Phil Wickham	
Psalm 119:105-112	Thy Word	Amy Grant	
Psalm 119:111	Endless Hallelujah	Matt Redman	

Psalm 119:1-16	Lord, I Have Made Thy Word My Choice	Issac Watts, Saint Michaels Singers	
Psalm 121	Song of Ascents	Birgitta Veksler	
Psalm 124	God Is On My Side	The Jackson Southernaires	
Psalm 136	Oh, How He Loves You and Me	George Beverley Shea	The Ultimate Collection
Psalm 139:1-2	Nothing Else + The Heart of Worship	Kari Jobe	
Psalm 139:1-3	You Are God Alone	Philips, Craig and Dean	
Psalm 139:14-16	You Are God Alone	Philips, Craig and Dean	
Psalm 139:7-12	You Are God Alone	Philips, Craig and Dean	
Psalm 141:2	You Are God Alone	Philips, Craig and Dean	
Psalm 145:18	You Are God Alone	Philips, Craig and Dean	
Psalm 146	Faithful Now	Vertical Worship	
Proverbs 3:5-6	Wonderful Peace	Fourhope	

Proverbs 16:20-33	Words	Hawk Nelson	Official Lyric Video
Ecclesiastes 3:9-15	My Story, Your Glory	Matthew West	Official Music Video
Isaiah 1:1-20	Clean Heart	Bryan and Katie Torwalt	
Isaiah 6:3	Holy, Holy, Holy	David Andrew	Album, 'Hymns'
Isaiah 41:8-10	Day By Day	Carolina Sandell Berg	Songs and Everlasting Joy
Isaiah 45:14-25	A King Like This	Chris Tomlin	
Isaiah 46:1-7	You Are God Alone	Philips, Craig and Dean	
Isaiah 49:16	You Are God Alone	Philips, Craig and Dean	
Isaiah 53	How Deep The Fathers' Love For Us	Collin Hill	
Isaiah 53:4-5a	Upon Him	Matt Redman	
Isaiah 53:5b	Jesus Paid It All	Josh Snodgrass	Acoustic Guitar
Isaiah 53:6	All We Like Sheep Have Gone Astray	Handels' Messiah	Toronto Symphony Orchestra
Isaiah 53:7	He Will Keep You	Sovereign Grace Music	
Isaiah 61	The King in All His Beauty	Sovereign Grace Music	

Jeremiah 36	Is He Worthy?	Chris Tomlin	
Lamentations 3:17-32	Great is Thy Faithfulness	Worship Refocus	Vocal arrangement
Ezekiel 1	Glorious	Chris Tomlin	
Ezekiel 2:1 & 2	Glorious	Chris Tomlin	
Daniel 7:9-28	Ancient of Days	Ron Kenoly	Integrity Music Live
Micah 6:6-8	Kindness	Steven Curtis Chapman	Official Lyric Video
Zephaniah 3:17	Endless Hallelujah	Matt Redman	
Matthew 4 1:11	My Weapon	Natalie Grant	Sacred version
Matthew 4:18-22	You Are My Strength	Reuben Morgan	Hillsong Worship
Matthew 5:14-16	Arise and Shine	New Wine	Official Lyric Video
Matthew 5:16	How Good is He	Vertical Worship	Song Sessions
Matthew 6:1-18	My Reward	Simply Worship/ Austin Ludwig	Official Lyric Video
Matthew 6:25-34	A Million Ways	Sanctus Real	Unstoppable God
Matthew 7:21-23	Nothing Else + The Heart of Worship	Kari Jobe	
Matthew 7:24-27	The Rock Won't Move	Vertical Worship	
Matthew 8:2-3	You Are God Alone	Philips, Craig and Dean	

Matthew 11:1-6	This We Know	Vertical Worship	
Matthew 15:11	Rumormill	Featuring Jon Mohr	Live
Matthew 19:24	Blessed	Vertical Worship	
Matthew 22:36-40	Lord, I Have Made Thy Word My Choice	Issac Watts, Saint Michaels Singers	
Matthew 24:35	You Are God Alone	Philips, Craig and Dean	
Matthew 26:6-13	The Great Exchange/The Girl Who Broke the Alabaster Jar	Sarah Liberman	The Invitation Version, Music Video
Mark 4:35-41	Jesus Calms the Storm	The Getty Girls	Keith and Kristyn Getty
Mark 6:30-34	Jesus, Full of Compassion	Caroline Cobb	2021
Mark 10:13-16	You Are God Alone	Philips, Craig and Dean	
Luke 4:16-21	The King in All His Beauty	Sovereign Grace Music	
Luke 4:29-30	The King in All His Beauty	Sovereign Grace Music	
Luke 14:16-30	Now is the Time	Evie	Mirror
Luke 14:25-33	Count the Cost	David Meece	

Luke 14:25-33	Worth It All	Brooklyn Tabernacle Choir	
John 1:1-18	My Weapon	Natalie Grant	Sacred version
John 1:14	My Weapon	Natalie Grant	Sacred version
John 1:29-34	This We Know	Vertical Worship	
John 2:1-12	Now is the Time	Evie	Mirror
John 3:17	The King in All His Beauty	Sovereign Grace Music	
John 4:5-30	How Majestic is Your Name	Sandi Patti	
John 6:1-13	How Majestic is Your Name	Sandi Patti	
John 7:6-8	Now is the Time	Evie	Mirror
John 8:20	Now is the Time	Evie	Mirror
John 8:31-32	The Truth Came Out	Peck Music Publishing	
John 10:1-30	The Good Shepherd	Tommy Walker Ministries	2017
John 12:1-8	The Great Exchange/The Girl Who Broke the Alabaster Jar	Sarah Liberman	The Invitation Version, Music Video
John 13:1	Now is the Time	Evie	Mirror
John 14:1-6	The Truth Came Out	Peck Music Publishing	
John 14:6	A King Like This	Chris Tomlin	

John 14:15-31	Standing on the Promise	The Georgia Mass Choir	Jaqueline Saunders, Savoy Records
John 14:31	Abide	Aaron Williams	Dwell Songs
John 14:25-27	Wonderful Peace	Fourhope	
John 15:1-11	Abide	Aaron Williams	Dwell Songs
John 15:14-16	Nothing Else + The Heart of Worship	Kari Jobe	
John 17:1-13	Now is the Time	Evie	Mirror
John 21:15-17	You Are My Strength	Reuben Morgan	Hillsong Worship
Acts 4:1-22	The Name of Jesus	Chris Tomlin	Lyric Video
Acts 17:10-12	. Thy Word	Amy Grant	
Romans 1:29-32	Honestly, We Just Need Jesus	Terrian	Official Music Video
Romans 6:23	His Robes for Mine	Hymns of Grace	Hymnology
Romans 7:14-25	Oh, What a Day	Stamps Baxter School of Music	2002
Romans 8:12-17	Oh, To Be Like Thee	Melissa Schworer	
Romans 8:26-30	Oh, To Be Like Thee	Melissa Schworer	
Romans 8:31-39	The Promise	The Martins	Above It All

Romans 8:34	How Majestic is Your Name	Sandi Patti	
Romans 12:12	Patience	The Music Machine	
Romans 12:12	Yes, I Will	Vertical Worship	Bright Faith, Bold Future
Romans 13:11-14	Honestly, We Just Need Jesus	Terrian	Official Music Video
1 Corinthians 3:4-9	Dream Small	The Stoltzfus Family	
1 Corinthians 5	Refiners' Fire	Brian Doerksen	It's Time
1 Corinthians 8:3	Nothing Else + The Heart of Worship	Kari Jobe	
1 Corinthians 10	Lord, I Need You	Matt Maher	All the People Said Amen, 2003
1 Corinthians 13	The Love of God	Guy Penrod	Blessed Assurance
1 Corinthians 15:1-4	It's About The Cross	The Ball Brothers	
1 Corinthians 15:1-5	I Believe	Phil Wickham	
1 Corinthians 15:50-58	It's About The Cross	The Ball Brothers	
1 Corinthians 15:51	Oh, What a Day	Stamps Baxter School of Music	2002
2 Corinthians 5:17	Oh, What a Day	Stamps Baxter	2002

		School of Music	
2 Corinthians 5:21	His Robes for Mine	Hymns of Grace	Hymnology
2 Corinthians 6:2	Now is the Time	Evie	Mirror
2 Corinthians 12:20	Honestly, We Just Need Jesus	Terrian	Official Music Video
Galatians 1:15	Nothing Else + The Heart of Worship	Kari Jobe	
Galatians 5:16-26	Hymn of the Holy Spirit	Pat Barrett	
Galatians 5:19-21	Honestly, We Just Need Jesus	Terrian	Official Music Video
Galatians 5:25	Lord, I Have Made Thy Word My Choice	Issac Watts, Saint Michaels Singers	
Galatians 6:1-2	Redeemer, Saviour, Friend	Keith Kitchen	Broomtree
Ephesians 1:3-9	Adoption Song	Brandon Lake	Lyric Video
Ephesians 2:18-22	Where I Belong	Building 429	
Ephesians 2:20-21	The Rock Won't Move	Vertical Worship	
Ephesians 4:25-31	Honestly, We Just Need Jesus	Terrian	Official Music Video
Ephesians 6:10-20	The Battle Belongs	Phil Wickham	

Ephesians 6:10-20	You've Already Won	Shane and Shane	Live
Epesians 6:16	Faith is the Victory	Josh Snodgrass	
Philippians 1:18-26	Celebrate Me Home	The Perrys	Official Live Video, Daywind Records
Philippians 2:14-15	Arise and Shine	New Wine	Official Lyric Video
Philippians 2:5-11	How Majestic is Your Name	Sandi Patti	
Philippians 2:9-11	A King Like This	Chris Tomlin	
Philippians 4	Wonderful Peace	Fourhope	
Colossians 1:19-23	I Believe	Phil Wickham	
Colossians 1:21-29	Call on the Name	Vertical Worship	
Colossians 3:17	My Story, Your Glory	Matthew West	Official Music Video
1 Thessalonians 2:19-20	Endless Hallelujah	Matt Redman	
1 Thessalonians 4:16-17	Endless Hallelujah	Matt Redman	
1 Timothy 1:15-16	Patience	The Music Machine	
1 Timothy 1:15-16	Yes, I Will	Vertical Worship	Bright Faith, Bold Future
Titus 3: 1-11	How Good is He	Vertical Worship	Song Sessions

Titus 3:1-7	Oh, What a Day	Stamps Baxter School of Music	2002
Hebrews 11	Stand in Faith	Danny Gokey	Official Lyric Video
Hebrews 11:1	Faith is the Victory	Josh Snodgrass	
Hebrews 12:1-2	Faith is the Victory	Josh Snodgrass	
James 1:19-25	Word of God, Speak	Mercy Me	
James 3	Rumormill	Featuring Jon Mohr	Live
James 3:13-18	Gentle Like Jesus	Sovereign Grace Music	
James 5: 16-20	Redeemer, Saviour, Friend	Keith Kitchen	Broomtree
1 Peter 2:11-12	Where I Belong	Building 429	
1 Peter 2:23	He Will Keep You	Sovereign Grace Music	
1 Peter 23:12	You Are God Alone	Philips, Craig and Dean	
1 Peter 4:1-5	Honestly, We Just Need Jesus	Terrian	Official Music Video
1 John 2:7-14	Lord, Shine Your Light	Elevating Gospel Worship	2004

1 John 3:19-24	Greater Than Our Hearts	Tom Mottershead	Official Lyric Video
3 John	Take My Life	Chris Tomlin	Passion
Revelation 4:8	Holy, Holy, Holy	David Andrew	Album, 'Hymns'
Revelation 5	All Glory	Vertical Worship	Song Sessions
Revelation 19:1-9	Symphony of Praise	Steve Green	Live
Revelation 21:1-7	Day By Day	Carolina Sandell Berg	Songs and Everlasting Joy
Revelation 21 + 22	I've Read the Back of the Book	The Cathedrals	

Manufactured by Amazon.ca
Bolton, ON

55278817R00127